Methuen Dram

Methuen Drama's *Modern Classics* series showcases landmark plays from around the world. Drawing on the *Modern Plays* series, which launched in 1959, *Modern Classics* celebrates plays from the contemporary repertoire by world-leading dramatists and presents their work in a definitive edition, alongside new introductions by leading scholars and industry professionals. With writers such as Pulitzer Prize-winners Jackie Sibblies Drury, Ayad Akhtar and David Mamet through to Lucy Prebble, Katori Hall and Caryl Churchill, *Modern Classics* are ideal for students and anyone wanting to deepen their knowledge of the plays that form part of the modern dramatic canon.

We Are Proud to Present a Presentation about the Herero of Namibia, Formerly Known as Southwest Africa, from the German Sudwestafrika, between the Years 1884 and 1915

A group of actors gather to tell the little-known story of the first genocide of the twentieth century. As the full force of a horrific past crashes into the good intentions of the present, what seemed a faraway place and time is suddenly all too close to home. Just whose story are they telling?

Pulitzer Prize-winning playwright Jackie Sibblies Drury collides the political with the personal in a play that is irreverently funny and seriously brave.

We Are Proud to Present... premiered off-Broadway at Soho Rep in 2012.

'A genuine THUNDERBOLT ... devastatingly funny ... dangerous and primal and weird.' *Washington Post*

'In recalling a traumatic chapter of African history, it magnifies the biases and conflicts that are inextricably part of the act of remembrance itself.' *LA Times*

This edition features an introduction by Leonor Faber-Jonker.

Jackie Sibblies Drury

Plays include *Marys Seacole* (OBIE Award), *Fairview* (2019 Pulitzer Prize), *Really, Social Creatures,* and *We Are Proud to Present a Presentation about the Herero of Namibia, Formerly Known as South West Africa, from the German Sudwestafrika, between the Years 1884–1915.* The presenters of her plays include Young Vic, Lincoln Center Theatre, Soho Rep., Berkeley Rep, New York City Players & Abrons Arts Center, Victory Gardens, Trinity Rep, Woolly Mammoth, Undermain Theatre, InterAct Theatre, Actors Theater of Louisville, Company One, and Bush Theatre. Drury has developed her work at Sundance, Bellagio Center, Ground Floor at Berkeley Rep, Soho Rep. Writer/Director Lab, New York Theatre Workshop, Bushwick Starr, LARK, and MacDowell Colony, among others. She has received the Susan Smith Blackburn Prize, a Jerome Fellowship at The LARK, a United States Artists Fellowship, a Helen Merrill Playwriting Award, and a Windham-Campbell Literary Prize in Drama.

We Are Proud to Present a Presentation about the Herero of Namibia, Formerly Known as Southwest Africa, from the German Sudwestafrika, between the Years 1884 and 1915

Jackie Sibblies Drury

With an introduction by Leonor Faber-Jonker

methuen | drama

LONDON • NEW YORK • OXFORD • NEW DELHI • SYDNEY

METHUEN DRAMA
Bloomsbury Publishing Plc
50 Bedford Square, London, WC1B 3DP, UK
1385 Broadway, New York, NY 10018, USA

BLOOMSBURY, METHUEN DRAMA and the Methuen Drama logo are
trademarks of Bloomsbury Publishing Plc

First published in Great Britain by Methuen Drama 2014
This edition published 2021

A catalogue record for this book is available from the British Library.

ISBN: PB: 978-1-3501-4640-2
ePDF: 978-1-3501-4641-9
eBook: 978-1-3501-4642-6

Series: Modern Classics

Typeset by Newgen KnowledgeWorks Pvt. Ltd., Chennai, India

To find out more about our authors and books visit
www.bloomsbury.com and sign up for our newsletters.

We Are Proud to Present a Presentation about the Herero of Namibia, Formerly Known as Southwest Africa, from the German Sudwestafrika, between the Years 1884 and 1915

by Jackie Sibblies Drury

Introduction

We Are Proud to Present… is a play about what we know, what we think we know and the limits of our understanding. Six young actors – half of them black, half white – attempt to present a presentation about the Herero of Namibia, the former colony of German South-West Africa (1884–1915). Inevitably, their presentation deals with genocide. Between 1904 and 1908, an estimated 80 per cent of the Herero and half the Nama population, a total of some seventy-five thousand men, women and children, lost their lives. They died at the hands of German soldiers, perished of thirst in the Kalahari Desert or were systematically worked to death in concentration camps. For decades, these atrocities were considered a mere 'colonial war'. Only in the twenty-first century has it been acknowledged that this was, in fact, a genocide, a systematic attempt to exterminate an entire people.

In what the *New York Times* described as her 'breakout work', playwright Jackie Sibblies Drury explores the many pitfalls of telling this history of colonial violence. *We Are Proud to Present…* is a play about making a play, on a topic fraught with ethical difficulties. The actors have done their homework: they read up on Namibia and the genocide and looked up the key dates of the history of German South-West Africa online. But then comes the hard part. How can they tell the story of the Herero when their only primary source material – a box of letters – is written by German soldiers? And who are they to speak for the Herero? Can a white actor play the part of a black Namibian, clinging to autonomy in an increasingly suppressive colonial state? Or a black actor the part of a German soldier? In beautifully structured dialogues, we follow the actors' confusion, discussion and conflict. Ultimately, this is an exploration of race, performance and representation.

Challenging the white space

We Are Proud to Present… introduced the Brooklyn-based playwright Jackie Sibblies Drury in 2012 as an exciting new voice in theatre, a voice as challenging and uncompromising as smart and entertaining. Since then, Drury's career has skyrocketed. Her follow-up play *Social Creatures* (2013) – an exploration of human nature in the guise of a zombie apocalypse – cemented her reputation, and in 2019, her latest play, *Fairview*, won the Pulitzer Prize for Drama. With a title referring to 'fair' as in 'just', and 'fair' as in 'white', *Fairview* was lauded as 'a hard-hitting drama that examines race in a highly conceptual, layered structure, ultimately bringing audiences into the actors' community to face deep-seated prejudices'. Ever since *We Are Proud to Present...*, Drury's work challenges theatre as a 'white space' by questioning the workings of theatre itself, the relationship between viewed and viewer, in intricate pieces laced with spiky humour.

Where issues of race and racism are often skirted around, Drury approaches these topics head-on. For her, not talking about these topics, or treating them as something 'already dealt with', is not an option. Playing with assumptions, perceptions and prejudices, her work makes the white gaze in theatre visible, *palpable*. *We Are Proud to Present...* is designed to make the viewer uncomfortable – in a productive way. That begins with the disturbingly essentialist introduction by the actors of their stage characters, who we get to know as Black Woman, White Man, Black Man, Another White Man and Another Black Man. Only the sixth character, a white German woman, has a name: Sarah. The actors are earnest, well-meaning, young, eager, a bit naïve. Unhindered by political correctness, or falling in its traps, they say and do things that are, as the stage notes indicate, '*not ok*'. Confronted with that, those things we have collectively decided not to do or say, we become aware of our own 'gaze', as betrayed by our reactions of laughter, irritation or unease.

In *We Are Proud to Present...* we never actually get to see the presentation about the Herero of German South-West Africa. After a stunted introduction, where the six actors fire facts at us, we join them in their rehearsal, gradually watching tensions build up as they share thoughts on how best to approach the subject. To 'figure out this whole genocide thing' (p. 78) they improvise, discuss, revisit. Egos clash, tempers flare. Finally, the play ends in a shocking culmination, when the boundaries between art and reality suddenly seem to dissolve. The audience is dragged into a frenzied scene that is as hard to watch as it is to act. Just like the actors presenting their presentation on the Herero, the performers playing the actors are faced with questions. *Is it right to say this? Can I be that person?*

Fairview (2019) is in many ways a counterpart to *We Are Proud to Present...*. Even more so than the latter, Drury's latest play is designed to make the audience uncomfortable. It starts with a cosy (if somewhat odd) scene featuring a black family, reminiscent of 1990s sitcom *Cosby*. In the next part, the entire scene is repeated, only now we can't hear the black family's dialogue. Instead, we hear the voices of white spectators – a straight white male, 'a flamboyant gay man, a French woman, and an American woman wary of offending anyone' – discussing the scene. Finally, the teenage daughter of the black family dramatically breaks the fourth wall by addressing the audience and asking those identifying as white to come onstage. Both *Fairview* and *We Are Proud to Present...* start with a rather misleading scene (the sugary sitcom; the fumbling actors presenting facts), followed by a middle part centred around a layered dialogue in which different voices are introduced that don't hold back, and a confrontational catharsis, a (direct) challenge to the audience.

By turning the tables, making certain sections of the audience uncomfortable to make space for people of colour, Drury reveals that the theatre (specific theatres excepted) is coded as a white space. The strength of her work lies in the way she does so, not by making demands, but by asking questions – either directed at the audience or implicit in the dialogues onstage. Questions that continue to resonate long after the curtains are drawn. That is why theatre critic Sara Holdren, who (like me) identifies as straight, white, cisgender, titled her discussion of Drury's last play 'Reviewing Fairview, a Play That Almost Demands That I Not Do So'. We all have our frames of reference, assumptions, prejudices. To challenge theatre as a white space, Drury forces you to reflect on them.

The extermination order

Writing *We Are Proud to Present...*, Drury never expected it to be produced at all, never mind it becoming a theatre sensation. Like many people writing about the Herero and Nama genocide (present author included), she happened on the topic while doing other research and felt compelled to work on it. It is astounding to learn about a German genocide preceding the Holocaust in a relatively little-known African country, to learn about the scale of the crimes committed there. The questions the actors grapple with are really questions Drury had when she started the project. Faced with the daunting task of writing about an African story, she decided to make a play about her own 'well-meaningness': the naïve need to tell the story of the genocide, and the doubts and uncertainties that come with that.

Like Drury, the actors have found most of their facts of Namibia and the genocide online. Introducing their presentation, they deal in quick succession with the languages of Namibia, before rambling through a year-by-year history of three decades of German rule in '*Südwestafrika*' between 1884 and 1915, when the Germans lost their colony to British-led troops from South Africa. They keep it clear and simple:

> **Actor 6**   1901.
>
> **Actor 1**   Germany tinkers a little with the law.
>
> **Actor 3**   If you are German and a cow wanders on to your land:
>
> **Actor 4**   It's yours!
>
> **Actor 3**   If you try to take a cow from a German and you aren't a German:
>
> **Actor 2**   You get hanged.
>
> **Actor 1**   Problem solved.

(p. 10)

And so the six actors continue in rehearsed staccato style, overtly simplifying colonial rule, but painfully grasping its essence: Germans did as they pleased, taking land and cattle at will. When the colony came under German rule in 1884, the Herero bore the brunt of the newcomers' unscrupulous ambitions. They owned huge herds of cattle and controlled the best grazing land, cradled between the Kalahari Desert to the east and the coastal Namib Desert to the west. To get a foothold in the colony, the Germans made use of their repeated conflicts with the Nama, a semi-pastoral people, by signing so-called 'protection treaties' (*Schutzverträge*) that promised protection of Nama raids and Herero retaliation. It soon turned out that it was, in fact, the Germans who the Africans needed protecting from.

From the very beginning of colonial rule, Germans treated black Namibians with blatant disrespect. Abuse was common, rape was standard. In the early days, the threat was relatively small, but as the influx of German settlers and soldiers increased in the 1890s, so did their disregard for the *Eingeborenen* ('natives'). In January 1904, a local 'uprising' of the Herero in Okahandja quickly spiralled out of control, setting the wheels of the genocide in motion. When the actors reach the years of the genocide, Actor 1 (White Man) intermits the summary of events (the Herero rebel; are taught a lesson; are made examples of; are chased into the desert; are imprisoned) with one repeated, harrowing sentence:

> **Actor 1**   The General issues the extermination order.
>
> (p. 11)

The word 'genocide' is not mentioned; that comes later, almost casually, as the actors discuss their progress. For now, this sentence says all there is to say. An order to *exterminate*. Issued by General Lothar von Trotha in October 1904, it warned the Herero:

> Within German borders every Herero, with or without a gun, with or without cattle, will be shot. I will no longer accept women and children, I will drive them back to their people or I will let them be shot at. (Gewald 1994, 68)

This *Vernichtungsbefehl* or 'destruction order' in fact condoned genocidal violence that was already happening. The first, damaging Herero attacks had provoked outright war fever. Losing to a 'racially inferior' enemy was deemed unacceptable and so Trotha was appointed, a general who had forged a reputation for ruthlessness in German East Africa. By the time he arrived in German South-West Africa, the majority of the Herero, some sixty thousand men, women and children, had conglomerated on the Waterberg plateau on the edge of the Kalahari Desert, where he encircled them, in order to deal them a decisive blow. When the Herero managed to flee in the direction of the desert (and British Bechuanaland beyond), Trotha ordered his men to give chase, driving the Herero ever deeper into the desert, away from waterholes. The 'order' made sure they stayed there. Thousands perished of hunger and thirst.

In the play, the actors mention a wall to keep the Herero in the desert (p. 11), but that would have been both unnecessary and impossible to build without African labour. In fact, the realization that valuable muscle power was being lost in the desert played a part in what followed. By the end of 1904, the *Vernichtungsbefehl* was revoked, only to be followed by the second, deadliest phase of the genocide. Surviving Herero, weak and emaciated, were rounded up from the desert, transported to concentration camps throughout the colony and forced to perform heavy labour, constructing railways and quays. Without adequate shelter or food, and suffering from disease and abuse, the prisoners died in droves. The Nama, who had taken up arms against the Germans in the final months of 1904, shared their fate. Those who survived never regained their freedom; their land was lost forever.

These are the bleak facts the actors are presenting.

Grave injustices that demand careful consideration, so as not to perpetuate them.

Violence between the lines

The raw facts of colonial rule in German South-West Africa summarized, the scene flows from presentation to rehearsal room, where the actors face the shortcomings of their primary source material: a set of letters by German soldiers. Problem is, these letters are silent about the vengeful violence, the rape and abuse, the killings. Instead, they speak of 'Home. Warmth. Comfort' (p. 18). Writing to their loved ones in Germany (*Liebe!*), the soldiers wrote about missing them, future plans and the unfamiliar land and people they encountered (p. 20). They describe the Herero, whom they observed as animals in a zoo, as 'tall and well muscled', 'more sociable and sweet tempered than … expected' (p. 31), carefully omitting any-thing harmful to the reputation of the German, 'civilized' soldier. It is their story, their viewpoint. Their gaze on the Other. Although the actors have doubts from the start, they try to work with the letters, until Actor 2 (Black Man) finally loses his patience:

Actor 2 Dear Sarah, Let me tell you some boring shit.

Actor 6 Come on –

Actor 2 Dear Sarah, You thought the last shit was boring? Well, you won't even believe how boring this new shit's gonna be.

Actor 6 Alright –

Actor 2 Dear Sarah, I'm killing black people every single day but I'm not going to tell you about that not when I can talk some more boring shit about your garden or your tree to your boring skinny arse.

(p. 52)

The contested letters are fictional. Rather than using actual letters, Drury has the actors discuss imagined correspondence that does illuminate the very real difficulties of working with colonial source material. In *Feldpostkarten* (field postcards) sent during the Herero and Nama genocide, the violence against Africans was rarely dwelled upon. It was either implicit or simply there. The postcards combined a short personal message with a photographic impression of the colony, usually flora or fauna, anonymous black Namibians ('heathen Herero' or *Negerkinder*) or idealized Germans on horseback, staring out into the distance. Some cards stand out for their more unscrupulous subject matter – captured Herero and Nama squinting into the camera, the execution of 'rabble-rousing murderers', colonial soldiers packing Herero skulls in a crate 'to be sent to German museums and institutes' – but even then, the messages on the back ('Happy Holidays!') are shockingly trivial, as light and meaningless as the letters read out by the actors.

Because the German letters are the point of departure for their presentation, the actors are faced with a problem. How to evoke violence if it is unspoken, implicit, glossed over by the writer? There is plenty of evidence of the genocide, from letters by General von Trotha detailing his intentions to skulls in European institutes and shallow graves in the desert, but the actors do not know this. They only have some facts, and the letters:

Actor 2   The letters don't have any evidence of anything
            happening to the Africans. They don't mention
            one prison camp, one hanging, one incident of –
Actor 1   So how do we know what even happened
            to them?

We –

Actor 2	**Actor 4**
So you're just saying	What do you mean how
that we just	do we know?
Made up the genocide?	

(p. 54)

Expressing doubts is treading on thin ice. That becomes even clearer
when Actor 5 (Sarah) makes the mistake of coming to the aid of Actor
1 with 'He's just saying that it's not like the Holocaust'. We know the
names of the six million people who perished in the Holocaust, she
hastens to add, but not those of the Herero (pp. 54–5). It's true. The
Herero were counted as 'heads', documented as numbers. That colonial context still influences our knowledge today, our understanding
of the genocide. There are, of course, Herero songs, Herero stories,
but these don't rank high when you google the genocide. And so,
the actors have a gap to bridge between the facts they looked up
(the 80 per cent death rate, the extermination order) and the sugary
letters about trees and gardens. Improvising the moment when the
extermination order comes into effect, the actors resort to a bitter
juxtaposition, where White Man (Actor 1) reads out another letter
to his 'Sarah' while firing shots at Black Man (Actor 2), punctuating
his lines with the pull of his trigger (pp. 77–8).

Not that type of Africa

Working, discussing, improvising in their rehearsal room, it
becomes obvious that the actors, determined to evoke the injustices
of the German colony, are far, far removed from the story they are
trying to tell. None of them have been to Africa, and they struggle
to imagine the Namibia described on Wikipedia. Reading about
the 'Hyper-Arid coastal plain' and the 'sub-Tropical High Pressure

Belt … providing more than 300 days of sunshine per year' is not the same as experiencing the sharp, merciless heat that seems to follow you like a searchlight, the gravelly landscape that stretches for miles in all directions, or the bone-chilling nights. Lacking such experiences, the actors have a hard time avoiding clichés when, fed up with the white perspective of the German letters, Actor 2 demands more 'Africa' in their African story:

> **Actor 2**   No no no. This is some
> *Out-of-Africa-African-Queen*-bullshit you all are pulling right here, ok?
> If we are in Africa, I want to see some black people.

(p. 41)

In response, Actor 4 (Another Black Man) dives into an improvisation involving a lush and green Africa, 'tiegahs' and 'jaguas'. As he gets carried away, he adopts a cringeworthy 'African' accent (stage note: *It's not ok*) while Actor 6 instigates a rhythmic 'African' drumming, picked up by Actors 1, 3 and 5. His improvisation becomes a shameless caricature of an African, polygamous, 'fertile as African jungle soil', feasting on raw meat. As the scene spirals out of control to the tune of frenzied drumming, Another Black Man becomes a character that seems to come straight from Joseph Conrad's *Heart of Darkness*, sucked in, spat out by the insanity of the bush. It is up to Actor 2 to stop the scene, bringing his colleagues back to reality, back to the facts:

> **Actor 2**   STOP.
> *They stop.*
> **Actor 2**   This isn't that kind of Africa.
> Ok?
> We already Wikipediaed this.

(pp. 43–4)

In a strange twist, the attempts of the actors to evoke an Africa they don't know echo the views of German soldiers and settlers on their new, unknown land. Fanciful ideas about wilderness and masculinity were eagerly projected on the new territory. By 1904, a generation of schoolboys had grown up with the immensely popular writings of author and fantasist Karl May, the adventures of Winnetou and Old

Shatterhand in the Wild West. For young German men, *Südwestafrika* was their very own 'American frontier', with its cattle farming, dry and hot landscape, alcohol-fuelled decision-making, and 'scrapes' with the indigenous, whose lives were worthless in the eye of the law. No wonder the idealized German on the field postcards is hard to distinguish from the archetypal cowboy, with his rifle and broad-brimmed hat, staring out across empty lands in a telltale echo of America's *tabula rasa* myth.

The similarities don't stop there. The frontier genocide in German South-West Africa and the genocide of the American Indians in California followed the same script. The pressure for land and resources, the dehumanization, the attack and retaliation, the final solution. Like their American counterparts, German adventurers felt entitled to rape, beat and murder the indigenous at will.

The actors don't mention such parallels, but they do draw from their own American(ized) frame of reference to come to an understanding of the racial violence in the colony. Drury wrote the play with American actors in mind, but also in Europe the notion of racial violence is informed by images that are distinctly American: the Hollywoodized whipping of a cotton plantation slave, grainy pictures of lynchings in the segregated South, the videotaped beating of Rodney King. When the actors improvise the scene following the issuing of the extermination order, White Man (Actor 1) shoots Black Man (Actor 2), calmly, inevitably, then continues shooting his fallen body (p. 77). The scene resonates with reports of police violence in the United States, where young black men are killed even when they're unarmed, even when they're just making their way home (p. 74). It is racial violence brought to its essence: Black Man breaks law (put in place by White Man), White Man shoots him.

They ain't your shoes

It must be clear by now: *We Are Proud to Present...* forces performers to go into a place they are incredibly uncomfortable with. After the improvised shooting of Black Man (Actor 2), Actor 1 is appalled by what his character has done. 'I can't do this,' he says, 'I can't – I'm not that person' (p. 78). Playing the part of White Man, he embodies all white men who ever hurt, suppressed, shot or murdered black men. It's a lot to take on his shoulders. The violent improv demands much of the actors in the play, and of the actual actors playing them. The German soldiers are people on the wrong side of history, people you don't want to relate to. For the white actors, even imagining what they talked about round the fire, what they wrote in their letters, is a bridge too far:

> **Actor 1**   It's history, there's facts, there's truth. I have no idea what it's really like to be someone like him. And I'm trying to figure out what kind of – who does something like – how someone can –
> **Actor 6**   So just be yourself, in his situation.
> **Actor 1**   But I'm nothing like him.
> **Actor 6**   You don't know that.
> **Actor 1**   Yes I do.

(p. 57)

Feeling the distance of time and space, they are constantly looking for ways to bridge these endless gaps, relating facets of the history of the Herero to their personal lives, their understanding of racial violence. In an attempt to understand 'how someone could do something horrible', Actor 3 (Another White Man) recalls a sensitive family history about his great-grandfather, who shot a black Union soldier during the American Civil War to save his own skin (p. 81). But his attempt is shrugged off by Actor 2, who is not interested in yet another 'white version' and points out it 'doesn't have anything to do with Africa' (p. 82).

Actor 3's story about his great-grandfather is ignored, but when Actor 6 makes a connection between the Herero and her own black British family, it is felt as real and significant. The physical resemblance between a Herero woman and her own grandmother – a woman who passed away before she was born – was her 'way in', she explains (p. 45). Her personal revelation is embraced by her fellow actors, both black and white, but perhaps not in the way she imagined, as one by one they act the part of the grandmother, bringing in their own ideas of British black identity to create this character, her accent, her expressions, her bulla cake recipe (p. 48). None of their representations are 'ok'.

Despite their best intentions, the actors' portrayals rarely venture past stereotypical. During the introduction of the presentation, the first, well-rehearsed part of the play, Black Man stiffly introduces Herero customs, the importance of land and cattle, ancestral fires. But he is talking to, being observed by the other actors. He is the Other, seen from a white perspective. When Actor 4 tries to imagine what it's like *to be* a Herero, he comes up with his tiger-killing jungle king. The German characters don't escape simplification either. Imagining Germanness, Sarah (Actor 5) bursts out in the Broadway-hit '*Edelweiss*' (p. 25). She adopts a corny German accent (Drury's stage notes: *It's not ok*) and introduces her children (two blond little men, obviously) Heiner and Leipzig, after the city in Eastern Germany (p. 33). Early-twentieth-century German life is as far removed from the actors as the Herero kindling their ancestral fires. Similarly, they come to realize they know as little about Actor 6's grandmother as about the Herero woman she resembles:

> **Actor 3** (*as Grandma*)   You better shut your mouth and listen to me, girl.
> You can't take no walk in somebody else's shoes and know anything.
> You ain't bought those shoes,
> you ain't laced those shoes up,
> you ain't put those shoes on day after day,
> you ain't broken those shoes in.
> Now, you can borrow somebody else's shoes, and
> you can walk as long as you want,
> they ain't your shoes.

(pp. 50–1)

The improvised appearance of the grandmother of Actor 6 raises another issue: can white Actors 3 and 5 get away with playing the black British grandmother of Actor 6? Or can only black people tell 'black' stories? This is an urgent question in all cultural domains, but perhaps, in the light of its painful blackface history, especially so in theatre. For Actor 2 (who does think he could pull off a convincing

German soldier) it is out of the question that his white co-actors can play the part of an African:

> **Actor 5**   We're finding the Herero in us.
> **Actor 2**   No, we're finding the Herero in *us* –
> **Actor 6**   We're all trying to find the Herero –
> **Actor 2**   You lot are finding Germans in you.
> **Actor 5**   Well, I don't only want to be a German.
> **Actor 2**   Too bad.
> **Actor 5**   I want to have another part.
> **Actor 2**   Well, you can't be an African.

(p. 64)

Similar to Actor 6 thinking Actor 1 must be able to imagine himself as a German soldier ('just be yourself in his situation'), Actor 2 equates being black with being African. In his view, the mutual experience of being black can connect here and there, then and now. And he has certain ideas about 'blackness', telling his black colleague Actor 4 off with 'That's not how black people talk' (p. 47). Pushing beyond history, beyond facts, here they come creeping back in, the sharp distinctions between 'black' and 'white', 'good' and 'bad', dichotomies we recognize from the *Feldpostkarten* sent by German soldiers, the pages of Karl May's novels. The six actors constantly correct each other, only to make new mistakes. *What do we know? How can we know?* Meanwhile, there's another nagging question: what would the Herero think of their play?

Stop, reread

In the above, I focused on three 'improvs' in the play: the shooting of Black Man by White Man, as the former attempts to get home when the extermination order is in place; the imagined Africa(n) of Actor 4; and the funny and outrageous interpretations of Actor 6's grandmother. These are three moments in the play where something shifts, something cracks. A white actor does not want to face the possibility that he could be that person, shooting down a fellow man in cold blood; lines are crossed ('*it's not ok*'), personal experiences blended in, crucial questions asked. In the conclusion of the play, these moments return, but now they are warped, grotesque, past uncomfortable.

It begins with a brief dialogue between Black Man (Actor 2) and Another White Man (Actor 3), similar to the one leading up to the shooting. They improvise the moment when new orders are given: to round up the Herero and imprison them. This time though, the dialogue is drowned out by violence, both verbal and physical. American slang seeps in: 'You don't talk back to me, *boy*'. 'You better run, *nigger*' (p. 92). The ugly bullying is set to the rhythm of chanting, reminiscent of the call-and-response songs of prisoners, slave songs to push monotonous work forward. Again, the actors get carried away in a rhythmic frenzy. But now, the heart of darkness truly catches up with them, in a scene haunted by questions asked earlier: can a white actor play the part of an African? White Man makes a crude white mask from one of the German letters and pushes it in front of Black Man's face, while impersonating him in the crudest possible way: 'Oooga booga!' (p. 93).

In the frenzy that ensues, all of Actor 2's earlier objections are smothered in an orgy of ugliness that almost results in the worst. As a reader, you stop and reread. *Are they really saying this?* As an onlooker, you flinch. *Are they really doing this?* The sharply funny dialogues have paved the way for a visceral, heart-wrenching ending. Reflecting on audience responses to *We Are Proud to Present...*, Drury said spectators might feel relief when, at the end, they don't have to look at a black person anymore. The final scene is the dehumanization of the Herero, the Jim Crow South and slavery rolled into one. It is the universal terrorizing of the Other. The facts are gone, but the truth remains. It is the history of the Herero in German South-West Africa brought to its very essence, the unimaginable horrors at the heart of colonial history made tangible through an onstage/offstage exploration of race and representation.

Leonor Faber-Jonker

Sources

Appel, Liz, 'Theater Is Coded as a White Space – Jackie Sibblies Drury Is Changing That', *Vogue*, 5 June 2019, https://www.vogue.com/article/jackie-sibblie-drury-fairview-pulitzer-interview.

Axster, Felix, '"…Will Try to Send You the Best Views from Here":
    Postcards from the Colonial War in Namibia (1904–1908)', in Volker
    M. Langbehn, ed., *German Colonialism, Visual Culture, and Modern
    Memory* (New York: Taylor & Francis, 2010).

Gewald, Jan-Bart, 'The Great General of the Kaiser', *Botswana Notes and
    Records* 26 (1994): 67–76.

Grady, Constance, 'Pulitzer Winner Fairview Is the Most Productively
    Uncomfortable Play I've Ever Seen', *Vox*, 15 April 2019, https://www.
    vox.com/culture/2019/4/15/18311873/2019-pulitzer-winner-drama-
    fairview-jackie-sibblies-drury.

Heaney, Christopher, 'Interview with Jackie Sibblies Drury: The Reenactors',
    The Appendix 1: 2, 12 June 2013, http://theappendix.net/issues/2013/4/
    interview-with-jackie-sibblies-drury-the-reenactors.

Holdren, Sara, 'Reviewing *Fairview*, a Play That Almost Demands That
    I Not Do So', *Vulture*, 17 June 2018, https://www.vulture.com/2018/06/
    reviewing-fairview-a-play-that-almost-demands-that-i-dont.html.

Interview with Jackie Sibblies Drury, InterAct Theatre Company, 17
    October 2013, https://www.youtube.com/watch?v=D6pkEYpoL3M.

Madley, Benjamin, 'Patterns of Frontier Genocide 1803–1910: The
    Aboriginal Tasmanians, the Yuki of California, and the Herero of
    Namibia', *Journal of Genocide Research* 6: 2 (2004): 167–92.

'*WE ARE PROUD TO PRESENT*... interview with Jackie Sibblies Drury
    and Gbolahan Obisesan', Bush Theatre, 21 February 2014, https://
    www.youtube.com/watch?v=m3efeYvcIA0.

We Are Proud to Present a Presentation about the Herero of Namibia, Formerly Known as Southwest Africa, from the German Sudwestafrika, between the Years 1884 and 1915

EMPATHY BY ANOTHER NAME

I heard this great theory about why cop shows are so popular . . .

Now when I say cop shows, I mean all those investigative/procedural/forensic/whodunit type of television shows; your *CSI*s, your *Law & Order*s, *Monk* if you like it quirky, *Prime Suspect* if you like it no-nonsense, or *The Bridge* if you like it Scandinavian.

Even though I really like this Cop Show Theory, I can't remember if it was originally uttered by a journalist or perhaps a cultural theorist, but the theory is so essentially true it must have been thought up by a comedian. The theory is:

Cop shows are popular because everyone wants to believe that someone is going to care about them after they're gone.

This philosopher-comedian would tell us that we all imagine that after we die a team of serious professionals – maybe charmingly gruff detectives, or impossibly beautiful scientists, or at least general but earnest and hard-working intelligent human beings – will work tirelessly, passionately, to find out *What Happened to Us*. To unravel the story of *How We Lived* and *How We Died*. Now this someone, perhaps in a lab coat, will at some point, in the midst of trying desperately to solve our untimely demise, bang a table and cry out:

She was a human being, dammit! She matters!

(Sob. Then quivering, yet steely.)

She. Mattered.

I imagine this impulse pre-dates the format of the television crime drama. I imagine that the impulse to be remembered, to make a mark, to matter, might be a criterion towards proving the evolution of a human consciousness. I think that this impulse's mate, the impulse to remember, to observe, to be affected, can be traced back to a the-chicken-or-the-egg-ishly similar genesis. For me, the artistic expression of these reciprocal impulses is theatre, and the elemental expression of these impulses is human-ness – empathy, by another name.

I think that this ancient impulse to remember and be remembered is a fierce and beautiful thing. It is why I am so drawn to history, to remembering, to studying how people have been remembered by other people, to wondering how people would like to be remembered, to imagining how other people may have remembered. This study helps me to feel my most human.

To study history is also, of course, to study death. While death is often considered a tragedy instead of an inevitability, when I am in the midst of feeling my most human, when I am remembering and wondering and imagining, I sometimes think that the most tragic death is the death that is elided over as history is canonised. That elided death doesn't participate in the process of metaphysical care that creates culture. It is not remembered, studied, imagined. That death is stripped of its humanity, which seems to be, if not a fate worse than death, perhaps a death worse than death. And perhaps, in turn, allowing that elided death to remain unimagined makes us a bit less human.

Jackie Sibblies Drury

ACKNOWLEDGEMENTS

I would like to thank: Mark Drury, Pat Sibblies, Eric Ting, Sandy Shinner, Geoffrey Jackson Scott, Sarah Benson, Caleb Hammons, Cynthia Flowers, Eric Ehn, Lisa D'Amour, Mallery Avidon, Mia Chung, Joe Waechter, Michael Perlman and Antje Oegel.

Jackie Sibblies Drury

WE ARE PROUD TO PRESENT. . . . was developed at the Magic Theater's Virgin Play Reading Series, the Bay Area Playwriting Festival/San Francisco Playwrights Foundation, Victory Garden Theater's Ignition Festival and received its world premiere in April 2012 at Victory Gardens Theater, Chicago, Illinois; directed by Eric Ting; Chay Yew, Artistic Director; Jan Kallish, Executive Director

WE ARE PROUD TO PRESENT . . . had its New York premiere at Soho Rep., Sarah Benson, Artistic Director, Cynthia Flowers, Executive Director.

WE ARE PROUD TO PRESENT . . . had its London premiere at the Bush Theatre in 2014 with the following cast and creative team:

Cast

Actor 6/Black Woman **Ayesha Antoine**

Actor 1/White Man **Joseph Arkley**

Actor 2/Black Man **Kingsley Ben-Adir**

Actor 3/Another White Man **Joshua Hill**

Actor 4/Another Black Man **Isaac Ssebandeke**

Actor 5/Sarah **Kirsty Oswald**

Creative Team

Director **Gbolahan Obisesan**

Designer **Lisa Marie Hall**

Lighting Designer **Azusa Ono**

Sound Designer **Donato Wharton**

Video Designer **Benjamin Walden**

Settings

A large space, a gathering place, a theater:

The presentation

In these sections, the performers have an awareness of the audience, or at least an audience. We see glimpses of a presentation, occurring in a theatrical space.

And a smaller space, a private place, a rehearsal:

The process

In these sections we see glimpses of a rehearsal through the fourth wall. The performers experiment without self-consciousness, rehearsing in the space without an audience, perhaps a bare-bones version of the actual space.

The presentation sections and the process sections are distinct at the start, but over time process becomes presentation, the spaces aren't what they appear to be and boundaries are broken.

The transitions between these sections should be quick and seamless. Each scene begins in the middle of things, and the play is performed continuously, cohesively, without breaks.

About the punctuation

A slash (/) indicates the interruption of the next line of text.

A set of brackets indicate that the line can either be spoken or, um, indicated.

Line breaks indicate a subtle, internal shift – not a pause.

A dash is an interruption – either by oneself or by someone else.

About the music

There is music in this text.

Music and rhythm should exist where they are indicated, and it should be added throughout.

About the time

One can think of the presentations scenes as glimpses from a longer and complete presentation, one that uses a variety of theatrical styles.

I've provided the years, roughly, that each scene is representative of. Or, we could say, the year in which the letter that is being presented was written. Please only use these years if/as they are helpful.

About the violence

The performance calls for real contact, as opposed to realistic contact. Actions that might make an audience wonder how they were done will work against the play. A slap to the shoulder, a loose rope around the neck: these things will feel much more dangerous than elaborate choreography or invisible rigging, in the end.

Characters

Actor 6/Black Woman

Actor 1/White Man

Actor 2/Black Man

Actor 3/Another White Man

Actor 4/Another Black Man

Actor 5/Sarah

All are young, somewhere in their 20s, and they should seem young, open, skilled, playful and perhaps, at times, a little foolish.

Note

This version of the text differs from the original American and has been adapted by the playwright for the European premiere at the Bush Theatre for a British cast.

Prologue

Intro, Lecture, Lecture/Presentation, Presentation

Actor 6 *enters.*

Actor 6   Sorry. We're all ready?

She greets the audience, probably with some warmth and casualness, definitely with some nervousness.

Actor 5 *hands her a stack of note cards.*

Actor 6   Great.

She glances at the cards, retrieves a pen and crosses 'Greet audience' off the list:

Actor 6 (*to herself*)   Greet audience. Fire speech.

She gives the fire speech, complete with cell-phone speech, etc.

Actor 6 (*to herself*)   Fire speech. Special announcements.

She makes any special announcements. She probably reads them off her papers/cards. If there are no theatre-related special announcements, perhaps there is a drinks offer at a nearby bar? A sale at the store down the street?

Actor 6 (*To herself.*)   Special announcements. Ok.

She reads a prepared speech. She also interrupts herself to clarify, talking directly to the audience. The lines that are read are italicized, the parts that are said are not.

Actor 6   *Hello. Thank you for coming.*
Oh, I already did that.
Welcome to our presentation.
We have prepared a lecture to proceed the presentation because we feel that you would benefit from some background information so as to give our presentation a greater amount of context.
Yeah. Ok, so, the lecture's a lecture but it's not a lecture lecture.
We made it fun.
Ish.

Sort of.

Anyway.

The lecture's duration should last approximately five minutes.
It might be ten. I'm bad at time.

Because, you know, what's happening is the important
thing, it doesn't matter when it happens, or how long it
happens for, it's that it's happening. Am I right?

(*Nervous laugh.*)

This is happening.

(*Nervous laugh.*)

Ok.

In this lecture – Um . . . Wait, what?

(*She flips through the cards.*)

Actor 5 *might try to feed her the lines.*

Actor 6   Ok.

(*To the ensemble and the audience at the same time.*)

'We' forgot to write in the part 'we' agreed 'we'd' write about
the overview.

So . . .

(*To the audience.*)

Ok. So, there's like a lecture that's only sort of a lecture and
then we did this thing that is kind of like an overview before
the lecture, which is before the presentation.

Does that make sense?

Ok.

Yeah . . .

I think I'm just going to skip some of this stuff, you know,
since it seems it doesn't actually say what we all agreed that it
should say. Even though we went through a lot to figure out
how to do this and introduce it properly, but this
introduction isn't what it's supposed to be so . . .

This is what we're doing: Lecture, Overview, Presentation.
Super fun, great.

(*To herself.*) Skip skip skip.

Helping me to present the lecture to you is our ensemble of actors.
Our ensemble of actors:

Actor 1   I'm an actor.

Actor 2   I'm an actor.

Actor 3   I'm an actor.

Actor 4   I'm an actor.

Actor 5   I'm an / actor.

Actor 6   *And I am an actor.*

Actors 1, 2, 3, 4, 5   Hello.

Actor 6   I'm also kind of the artistic director of our ensemble, so. Okay.

In this presentation, which has already started, I know, *I will be playing the part of Black Woman. I am also black, in real life, which you might find confusing. Please try to think of it like this: Black Woman is just the name of the character I'm playing.*

This actor will be referred to as Black Man.

This actor will be referred to as White Man.

This actor will be referred to as Another Black Man.

This actor will be referred to as Another White Man.

This actor will – (*To* **Actor 5**.) Actually, we haven't really explained you yet. And they won't get it, so . . . (*To the audience*.) Just ignore her for right now. Ok.

Another White Man . . . because this is true in real life and in this lecture and subsequent presentation.

Now, without further ado, we present to you a lecture about Namibia. (A lecture shared by the group: a map, a Powerpoint presentation.)

A lecture about Namibia.

Located in the southern most section of the African continent, Namibia is bordered by: Angola, Zambia, Botswana, Zimbabwe, South Africa, and the Atlantic Ocean. Let me repeat that. Or – you guys get it: Blah, blah, blah, blah, blah, and the Atlantic Ocean.

Some other facts about Namibia. Namibia's official language is English:

Actor 4   Hello.

Actor 6   *Namibia's recognized regional languages are Afrikaans:*

Actor 1   Hallo.

Actor 6   *Oshiwambo*:

Actor 2   Ongiini.

Actor 6   *and German:*

Actor 3   Guten Tag.

Actor 6   *There is a reason for this. An historical reason.* This is really what the lecture is about. *An explanation for the recognized languages in Namibia. Let us begin with Oshiwambo.*

Actor 2   Oshiwambo –

Actor 6   *Oshiwambo is spoken by a tribe called the Herero:* The Herero:

Actors 1, 2, 3, 4, 5 (*to the audience, with a helpful smile*)   The Her-er-oh.

Actor 6   Actually, Oshiwambo was originally spoken by the Ovambo people, but we aren't really talking about them at all so . . . The Herero.

Actors 1, 2, 3, 4, 5   The Herero.

Actor 6   *Another of Namibia's languages is English –*

Actor 4   English.

Actor 6   *English is spoken in Namibia because the British expanded their colonial holdings during World War I –*

Actor 3   – World War I.

Actor 6   *That is the reason why English is spoken in Nambia. The third of Namibia's languages is Afrikaans –*

Actor 1   – Afrikaans –

Actor 6   *– Afrikaans is spoken in Namibia because Afrikaans speakers needed to expand their ranches into Namibia settling permanently around the turn of the nineteenth century –*

Actor 4   – that's 1900?

Actor 6   1800.
(*The slide is wrong.*)

Actor 5   Oh, fuck.

(*She fixes the slide.*)

Actor 3   1800.

(Ok. Now they start to get it together. They're getting into the section that they rehearsed the most.)

Actor 6   *Around the turn of the nineteenth century, before Namibia became a German colony:*

Actor 1   Sudwestafrika!

Actor 6   *– which is the name for the colony in German –*

Actor 4   Oshindowishi!

Actor 6   *– which is the name for German in Oshiwambo. Namibia became a German colony in 1884. It stopped being a German colony in 1915, when it was taken by the British:*

Actors 1, 2, 3, 4   During World War I!

Actor 6   *– but between 1884 and 1915, when Namibia was –*

Actor 1   Sudwestafrika!

Actor 6   *– which is where –* which is when? *–*

Actor 5   *disagrees with her 'when', saying 'where'.*

Actor 6   *Which is when we are concentrating today. We have access to*:

Actor 4   Postcards!

Actor 1   Karte!

Actor 5   Letters!

Actor 3   Stukken van Document!

Actor 2   Ombapila!

Actor 6   – *a cache of letters from German troops stationed in German South West Africa between the years 1884 and 1915.*

But before we present the presentation of those letters, we have the overview.
Which we don't have an introduction for. So.
This is going to be the overview.
Or, should we say it?

The **Actors** *agree: 'Yeah' or 'I guess?' or 'Yes, yes, keep going.' Etc.*

Actor 6   Yeah – let's all say it together.

A fast-paced cartoonish overview – a romp. They've like actually really memorised this part. They move through it very quickly, at times frantically.

If they have simple puppets/illustrations/costumes, **Actor 5** *made the puppets/illustrations/costumes. There's probably slapstick, a pratfall, some high jinks.*

The announcement of each year is preceded by a sound: punctuation, the ding of a bell. And with each ding, a brief comic tableau that sums up what was said about the previous year.

All   An overview of German South West Africa between the years 1884 and 1915.

Actor 6   1884.

Actor 1   Germany is in charge.

Actor 3   Sort of. All the tribes are actively not saying they hate us.

Actors 2 and 4   Hey Germany. We aren't *saying* we hate you.

Actor 6   1885.

Actor 2 Agreements are reached with tribal leaders –

Actor 1 Germany is totally in charge.

Actor 2 Well, some of the tribal leaders.

Actor 6 1886.

Actor 1 Germany is like actually in charge.

Actor 3 Germany is telling other people that they're in charge.

Actor 1 Germany is like basically actually in charge.

Actor 6 1887.

Actor 1 The Germans are impressed by one tribe in particular, the Herero.

Actors 2, 3, 4, 5 The Her-er-oh.

Actor 6 The Herero.

Actor 2 So tall.

Actor 4 So muscular.

Actor 1 The Germans put –

Actors 2, 3, 4, 5 The Her-er-oh.

Actor 1 – in charge of all / the tribes –

Actor 6 The Germans put the Herero in charge of all the tribes in German South West Africa.

Actors 2 and 4 Hurray!

Actor 6 1888.

Actor 2 The Herero are in charge.

Actor 3 Sort of.

Actor 6 1889.

Actor 1 The Germans are kind of over the Herero.

Actor 3   Over the Herero.

Actor 2   So childish and ungrateful.

Actor 4   So impudent and unwashed.

Actor 6   1890.

Actor 1   The Germans put the Hottentots –

Actor 3   The Nama.

Actor 1   The Nama in control. The Germans give a bunch of Herero cattle to the Nama.

Actor 3   Herero cattle to the Nama.

Actor 2   Which, like sucks.

Actor 4   Because the Herero love their cows.

Actor 2   We do.

Actor 6   1891.

Actor 1   The Germans are sort of over the Hotten – Nama.

Actor 3   Over the Nama.

Actor 6   1892.

Actor 1   The Germans put the Herero back in control. They give a bunch of Nama cattle to the Herero.

Actor 3   Nama cattle to the Herero.

Actor 4   Which is sort of stealing.

Actor 2   But they were our cows to begin with.

Actor 6   1893.

Actor 4   The Nama fight the Herero.

Actor 2   The Herero fight the Nama.

Actor 1   The Germans take the cattle –

Actor 3   – take care of the cattle –

Actor 1   – care for the cattle –

Actor 6   1894.

Actors 1, 2, 3, 4, 5   Tenuous peace.

Tableau: Tenuous peace. Smile: ding!

Actor 6   1895.

Actor 1   The Germans decide to build a railroad into the interior.

Actors 1, 2, 3, 4, 5   More resources for everyone.

Tableau: Fiscal success. Bigger smile: ding!

Actor 6   1896.

Actor 1   We are building that railroad.

Actor 3   We are building that railroad.

Actor 2   *We* are building that railroad.

Actor 6   1897.

Actor 1   We are failing.

Actor 3   We are failing.

Actor 2   We are building that railroad.

Actor 6   1898.

Actor 1   We are really failing.

Actor 3   Not good.

Actor 2   We are building that railroad.

Actor 6   1899.

Actor 1   We are fucked.

Actor 3   So fucked.

Actor 2   We are building that fucking railroad.

Actor 6   1900.

Actor 1   German settlers are getting poorer and poorer –

Actor 3   – and madder and madder, and the German government –

Actor 1   – is getting madder and madder and poorer and poorer.

Actor 3   Because of the fucking railroad.

Actor 2   We are building that –

Actor 6   1901.

Actor 1   Germany tinkers a little with the law.

Actor 3   If you are German and a cow wanders on to your land:

Actor 4   It's yours!

Actor 3   If you try to take a cow from a German and you aren't a German:

Actor 2   You get hanged.

Actor 1   Problem solved.

Actor 6   1902.

Actor 1   Germany tinkers a little more with the law.

Actor 3   If you are German and you see land that doesn't belong to a German:

Actor 4   It's yours!

Actor 3   If you contest a German land claim and you aren't German:

Actor 2   You get hanged.

Actor 3   If you are German and you see cattle on the land you have just claimed:

Actor 4   The cattle are yours!

Actor 3   If you steal cattle from a German and you aren't German:

Actor 2   You get hanged.

Actor 6   1903.

Actor 4   The Nama rebel against German rule.
It doesn't end well.

Actor 3   But it does end quickly.

Actor 6   1904.

Actor 2   The Herero rebel against German rule.

Actor 1   The Herero are taught a lesson.

Actor 3   The Herero are made examples of.

Actor 1   The General issues the extermination order.

Actor 6   1905.

Actor 1   The General issues the extermination order.

Actor 3   The Germans imprison thousands of Herero in labour camps.

Actor 6   1906.

Actor 1   The General issues the extermination order.

Actor 3   The Germans force thousands of Herero into the desert.

Actor 6   1907.

Actor 1   The General issues the extermination order.

Actor 3   The Germans erect a wall to keep them in the desert.

Actor 6   1908.
The extermination order has been issued.
The labour camps have closed.
Eighty per cent of the Herero have been exterminated.

Those that survived the camps
were used as a source of unpaid labour by the German
settlers.
And in this way, the German regime continued:
1909
1910
1911
1912
1913
1914
1915.
And then. And only then do the British intervene.

Actor 3   World War I.

Actor 6   And there you have it.
A history of German colonial rule in Namibia.

Big finish:

The formal beginning to the presentation.

All   We Are Proud to Present a Presentation About the
Herero of Namibia,
Formerly Known as South-West Africa, From the German
Sudwestafrika,
Between the Years 1884 and 1915.

Scene: Process

And bam: we're in the rehearsal room.

*The mood is instantly more casual, but no one takes a breath because
everyone is speaking quickly, overlapping, interrupting, having
multiple convos at once, moving things around, getting a snack,
checking his phone, consulting the research, etc., etc., etc.*

Actor 6   And, what if we ended it right there?

Actors 1/2/3/4   What? / Wait. / Whoa. / Umm . . .?

Actor 5   Why?

Actor 6   Because. I don't know if we actually need to read the letters.

Actors 1 and 5   Why not.

Actor 6   I think the overview might be enough.

Actor 5   But what about my song?

Actor 1   I thought the presentation was presenting the letters.

Actor 4   That's what we're doing, aren't we?

Actor 6   I don't think we should present the letters.

Actor 5   You always do this.

Actor 6   Do what?

Actor 3   Oh come on.

Actor 1   You always kind of . . . take over?

Actor 6   I'm not taking over.

Actor 5	**Actor 3**
I want to read the letters.	You're kind of taking over.

Actor 4   I thought that was what we were doing.

Actor 6   Have you read them?

Actor 1	**Actor 5**
I've read them.	Yes.

Actor 3   Me too.

Actor 2   All of them?

Actor 1	**Actor 5**
Most of them.	Yes.

Actor 6   I don't think we should just stand there and / read these letters.

Actor 1 (*to* **Actor 6**)	**Actor 5**
We're not going to just	But I've read the
stand there	letters and

Actor 3 (*to* **Actor 6**)   I don't know if this is your decision to make.

Actor 1 (*to* **Actor 6**)   It's theatre, you know? / You don't just stand there.

Actor 5 (*to* **Actor 6**)   I thought we were an ensemble.

Actor 6 (*to* **Actor 5**)   We *are* an ensemble.

Actor 2 (*to* **Actor 1**)	**Actor 5**
So then –	Well, it's a presentation,
	its's not theatre.

Actor 6 (*to* **Actor 3 and Actor 5**)   And as a member of our ensemble / I think I have the right to express an opinion.

Actor 1 (*to* **Actor 2**)   But it's a presentation in a theatre.

Actor 2	**Actor 3**
(*to* **Actor 1**)	(*to* **Actor 6**)
Right.	Right.

Actor 1   So it's theatre.

Actor 4 (*to* **Actor 1**)   Well I don't know if it is.

Actor 3	**Actor 1**
You should absolutely	What?
express an opinion.	

Actor 6   I know.

Actor 4   I don't know if it's theatre just because it's *in* a theatre.

Actor 5   And I have the right to express my opinion too, don't I?

Actor 6	**Actor 1**
Yes, you can –	Wait, what?

Actor 3   This is what I'm saying.

Actor 2 (*to* **Actor 4**)   He's not asking like theoretically, he's actually *asking*.

Actor 3 (*to* **Actor 5**)   Why are you asking her for permission to express an opinion?

Actor 4 (*topping everyone*)   Ok, but, regardless, whatever it is that we're trying to do, I don't understand why we're not reading the letters.

Actor 5 (*to herself – a grumble?*)   I'm not asking anyone for permission.

Actor 3   Well, not all of us are saying that we're not reading the letters.

Actor 6   I am saying that I think that the letters are.

Actor 3   What?

Actor 6   Ok. I'm saying that I think that they're all . . . kind of the same.

Actor 1	**Actor 3**	**Actor 4**
No way.	Oh come on.	Really?

Actor 5   But they're by different people.

Actor 6   They're all soldiers.

Actor 5   Yeah, different soldiers.

Actor 6   They're all German soldiers and I'm saying like dramatically they're all doing the same thing.

Actor 5   But I had to like *pick them up.*

Actor 6	**Actor 1**
I know.	I think that they're different.
Actor 5	**Actor 2**
Like at the *library.*	They aren't that different

Actor 6 And it's amazing that you found them	**Actor 1** But they're different people.
Actor 5 Like the *weird* part of the library.	**Actor 4** Different people doing the same thing isn't that different.

Actor 6   I just don't think we should present them.

Actor 2   I don't think so either.

Actor 1 You didn't even read them.	**Actor 5** Seriously?
Actor 2 I read some of them.	**Actor 6** It's like letter after letter / soldier after soldier —

Actor 1   But they're / the whole centre of the piece – I just don't understand why we wouldn't use them.

Actor 3   Shouldn't / we try something out? Before we just –

Actor 5   But every person is special, can't we agree that every person is –

Actor 4   But if we aren't going to read the letters what are we going to do?

Actor 3   I really think we should read the letters.

Actor 6   Fine. Ok.
You want to read the letters?
Let's read alllll of the letters. Right now.
And then we can decide.

Actor 5   Great. Here.

Actor 1   Dear – um – uhhh.

Actor 6   Read it.

Actor 5   He's reading it.

Actor 1   I don't know how to pronounce this.

It doesn't say Sarah.

Actor 6   Sarah.

Actor 1   But it's not an S – it's like a –

Actor 6   Just say Sarah. Read the letter.

Actor 5   Just say Sarah.

Actor 1   Dear Sarah – Dear Sarah,
I miss you like the July sapling misses April rains. And I –

Actor 6 (*sound of disgust*)

Actor 1   But –

Actor 6   Seriously (*another sound of disgust*).

Actor 5   But I think –

Actor 6   Don't you see what I'm talking about?

Actors 1 and 5   No.

Actor 6   It's just so. There's like no violence, there's no
anger there's no –

Actor 5   Well, it's just like the beginning of –

Actor 3   What about this one?
Ok. Dear – um –

Actor 6   Just say it's Sarah.

It really doesn't say Sarah.

Actor 3   I really don't think it's pronounced –

Actor 6   They're all the same – the names aren't important.
Let's just say they all start Dear Sarah. Okay?

Actor 5   Fine. All the women are Sarah.

Actor 3   But –

Actor 6   Just read it.

Actor 3   That doesn't –

Actor 5   Just read it.

Actor 3   Ok. God.
Dear Sarah –

Actor 5   Oh my God.
Wait, can I be Sarah?
No – I'm Sarah.

Actor 3   Oh – ok.

Actor 5   I am Sarah.

Actor 3   Um. Right, ok.
Dear Sarah,
Once night has fallen, I look to the sky and think of you.
The stars are –

Actor 6   Just like the other ones.

Actor 5   No it's not –

Actor 4   Wait wait wait – ok guys – listen to this – Dear –

Actor 6   Sarah.

Actor 5   I'm Sarah.

Actor 4   I know. Dear Sarah, it has been so long since –

Actor 6   Blah blah, miss. Blah blah, love.

Actor 1   Dear Sarah,

Actor 5   I'm Sarah.

Actor 1   Tell me of our little –

Actor 6   Blah blah. Children. Family. Who cares?

Actor 3   Dear Sarah, The camp is not –

Actor 6   Home. Warmth. Comfort. They're all the same.

Actor 4   Dear Sarah, We have been apart for so long –

Actor 6   Whatever. Distance. They're all the same.

Actor 5   No they're –

Actor 6   They're basically all the same.

Actor 5   Sure, basically, but –

Scene: Presentation [1884]

Actor 6   Here we have White Man:

White Man   Guten Tag.

Actor 6   A young German soldier
leaving the mining town of Zwickau for the first time
Travelling for miles and miles –

Another White Man   – kilometres and kilometres –

Actor 6   Travelling with thousands and thousands of fellow
soldiers:

Another White Man   Guten Tag.

Actor 6   And they travel for weeks
Over land
Over sea
Until finally they arrive at their new home:

White Man *and* **Another White Man**   Sudwestafrika.

Actor 6   And survey their new territory.
To the north:

White Man   The interior.

Sarah   Das innenraum.

Another White Man   Land and materials to be discovered
and developed and exported

Actor 6   To the south:

White Man   The pasture.

Sarah   Die weide.

Another White Man   Prairie, grasses as far as the eye can
see, grazing lands for millions of cattle.

Actor 6   To the east:

White Man   The desert.

Sarah   Die wüste.

Another White Man   Kilometres and kilometres.

White Man   And miles and miles.

Another White Man   Dry, hot, arid, barren.

White Man   Unforgiving and inhospitable.

Actor 6   And to the west:

White Man   The ocean.

Sarah   Der ozean.

Another White Man   The ocean.

Actor 6   And all of this:

White Man *and* **Another White Man**   Sudwestafrika.

Actor 6   Is now considered Germany.

Sarah   Deutschland.

Actor 6   And from this place that is so unfamiliar,
That has been given the name of his home,
Our young German soldier:

White Man   Guten Tag.

Actor 6   Writes a letter to his young wife, Sarah:

Sarah   Ach! Liebe!

Actor 6   Who waits for him, back in his familiar home,
A home he many never see again:

White Man   Dear Sarah.
Today is the first of many days
I will spend away from you.
I will travel far away today.
I will post this letter if I arrive –

I will arrive, and
I will post this letter to you.
I will think of you always, and
I will be my best, so that
I will know that when I return
I will be the man you have imagined
I will become.

Scene: Process

Actor 6   Great. Wow – Really great.
Moving on.

Actor 1   Wait –

Actor 6   What?

Actor 1   Well, I kind of need to process that?

Actor 6   Process what?

Actor 1   It's just, I sort of dived in, you know?

Actor 6   Ok . . .

Actor 1   And it's like, I know that I found something,
something real, but it's like, I'm not sure what came across,
or –

Actor 5   I thought it was kind of sad.

A passive-aggressive, fake helpful exchange.

Actors 1 *and* **Actor 5** *have had this fight before . . .*

*Whatever. Each actor thinks he/she is being the bigger person by
helping the other, who is a total idiot.*

Everyone else should want to climb out of a window.

Actor 1   Sad? Really?

Actor 5   *Kind* of.
Don't worry, we'll find it in improv.

Actor 1   No, but I think he's being romantic.

Actor 5   Is he?

Actor 1   Yeah.

Actor 5   Really?

Actor 1   Yeah.

Actor 5   Huh.

Actor 1   He's being romantic and it's like he's reassuring her.

Actor 5   Oh, I see.

Actor 1   You get it?

Actor 5   Totally.
Just, a question?

Actor 1   Sure.

Actor 5   Why does *she* need to be reassured?

Actor 1   Why?

Actor 5   Yeah.

Actor 1   Um, isn't that kind of obvious?

Actor 5   I don't think it is, actually.

Actor 1   Well, it's like I thought since he was going to this like distant land, and stuff, that she would be worried about him, you know?

Actor 5   Hmm –

Actor 1   But that's just one idea.

Actor 5   Yeah –

Actor 1   Like I know if someone that I loved was going off to maybe *die* I'd be like, worried.

Actor 5   Totally.

Actor 1   Right?

Actor 5   I totally agree.

Actor 1   Yeah.

Actor 5   But I'm just wondering why you're like *assuming* that she's the only one who's worried.

Actor 1   I'm not assuming anything.

Actor 5   No, you kind of are, I think?

Actor 1   Ok.

Actor 5   I'm just saying maybe he should be worried.

Actor 1   Great. Well, thanks for the *note* –

Actor 5   Ok.

Actor 1   But I think I got it.

Actor 5   You know what?
All I was trying to say was that your reading didn't totally work for me.
That's all.
But I'm only one person. What did everybody else think?

Actor 6   I thought it was fine.

Actor 5   You did.

Actor 6   I thought it was romantic.

Actor 1   I thought so too.

Actor 6   And scared.

Actor 1   Scared.

Actor 6   Yeah, like he was scared.
He doesn't know what he's facing, he's going to this crazy place that is so different from where he grew up –

Actor 3   I keep hearing that this guy is going to this place that is *so different*.
But what *I'm* wondering is *where* he grew up.
Like *what* is this *different place* so *different from*.

Actor 6   That's a good point.

Actor 3   And it's like, from what you guys have been talking about it's like I think I'm going to be like the Best Friend right?

Since you know.

It seems like a decision has already been made that he's the leading man.

Actor 6   Oh, I don't know that we've decided that.

Actor 3   No no it seems like you *did* decide that *and* it seems like pretty final. So.

It's fine.

I'm just trying to get a sense of where I'm building my Best Friend character from. I'm perfectly comfortable with a character part. Obviously.

Actor 1   You're so good at character roles.

Actor 3   I know. I do. I know I am.

So. Where did he grow up?

Actors 6 *and* **1**   Germany.

Actor 3   No, *where*. *Where*. The *streets*, the *city*. The *smells*, the *quality of light*.

Now, for my part, I know that I grew up in . . . Cologne.

Actor 2   They pronounce it Köln in German.

Beat.

Actor 3   I though we weren't doing accents.

Actor 6   We're not.

Actor 3   Because I can do a German accent. I have / access to several regional accents in Germany, several –

Actor 6   We aren't doing accents / we agreed that we aren't doing accents.

No accents.

No one is doing an accent.

We don't need the song.

We don't need the accents.

Oh my God.

Actor 5   I can do a great / Edelweiss:

Actor 5 *sings, nay performs, Edelweiss. Everything is a kind of cacophonous mess.*

Actor 2   All I'm saying is if he was from Cologne, wouldn't he call it Köln?
Why would he call it Cologne / if he was from Cologne.

Actor 3   Because he's not a German German, but he's basically German.

Actor 2   If you didn't know that Köln was the right / way to say Cologne
there's no shame in that.
I don't know that you knew that.
I know that Cologne is Köln but I'm not sure that you knew Cologne is Köln.
I know we aren't doing accents
I know we aren't doing accents because
I can do a German accent
I can do an African accent
I can do an African accent while speaking German: Ich bin ein Berliner.

Actor 3   Of course I knew that: Cologne is Köln Cologne is Köln.
Everybody knows that. But we aren't doing accents
I'm not doing a German accent
You aren't doing an African accent
We aren't doing accents
We aren't doing accents because
if we were doing accents I would be doing an excellent German accent
A regional Rhineland accent: Spreken-ze deutsch?

Actor 6   Are you finished?

Big finish for **Actor 5**'*s Edelweiss.*

Actor 6   Are you finished?
Because that isn't what this is about.
It's about.

Actor 1   It's about touching something real.

Actor 5   Like a raw nerve.

Actor 1   No, something real.

All think about reality.

Actor 5   Like, the horror of our capacity to casually inflict suffering.

Actor 1   Well –?

Actor 6   Alright. So make it real.
Let's go back to the letter.
Take it from 'I will be my best –' when you're ready.

Actor 1   Great.
But.

Actor 6   Yes?

Actor 1   I'd like to take it from a little bit before that just because well it's like in the middle of –

Actor 6   Great. Take it from wherever you need. When you're ready.

Actor 1   Great.

I will think of you always, and
I will be my best, so that
I will know that when I return
I will be the man you have imagined
I will become.

Actor 6   Great.
Ok. Sarah – what's going on with you?

Actor 5   He's not – I mean I'm trying to be sad
but he's not giving me anything to work with.

Actor 1   But I think the letter is supposed to be romantic –

Actor 6   We're working with Sarah right now White Man.
Now, Sarah.

Actor 5   Yes.

Actor 6   When I'm sad, I always end up thinking about the same thing.
Do you have something like that, Sarah?

Actor 5   I think of my cat.

Actor 6   Your cat?

Actor 5   He's dead.

Actor 6   That's sad.

Actor 5   Yes it is.

Actor 6   Great.
Let's go into the cat.

Actor 5   Really?

Actor 6   Yes.
White Man – give us the end again.

Actor 5 *goes into her memory. She is very focused.*
She doesn't think about her cat, she becomes The Cat.

White Man   I will think of you always, and
I will be my best, so that
I will know that when I return
I will be the man you have imagined
I will become.

Actor 6   Great. Sarah.

Actor 5 *is still The Cat.*

Actor 6   Sarah.
Ok, I think we might need to . . . push that memory. Ok?

Actor 5   But I thought –

Actor 6   No, you're doing great.
Ok. I want you to think of your cat as though it were still alive today.

Actor 5   But he couldn't be. He'd be like a jillion years old.

Actor 6   Well, wouldn't you know it,
the saddest thing that I have ever seen was a really old cat.

This is probably a lie.

Actor 5   Really?

Actor 6   Yup. It was horrible.
It had arthritis.
I could see its knotted stiffened joints.
It didn't move like a cat.
It couldn't jump.

Actor 5 (*sad face* ☹)

Actor 6   It couldn't stalk.

Actor 5 (☹)   Aww –

Actor 6   It could only eat and shit and cry.

Actor 5 (☹☹)   Aww noo.

Actor 6 (*needing to go further*)   It was missing an eye.

Actor 5 (*actually horrified*)   Oh my God.

Actor 6   More than missing.
One of its eyes was already dead. Decomposing.
It would open its mouth to lick at its decomposing eye
And cry 'Feed me or kill me'.

Actor 5   Oh my God.

Actor 6   It would look me dead in the eye – with its one
good eye –
and watch me watch it make
yet another agonizing shuffle towards food or death.
And it would gather its remaining strength
to cry 'Feed me or kill me'.

Actor 5   Oh God.

Actor 6   And I could do neither.
I could not show the cat kindness.
I was too sad. It made me too sad.
How do you feel?
Sarah, how do you feel?

Actor 5   So sad.

Actor 6   Great. Hold on to that.
Let's do another letter.

Actor 1   Do you have anything for me?

Actor 6   Just keep doing what you're doing.

Actor 1   Great.

Actor 6   Great.

Scene: Presentation [1887]

Actor 6   Here we have Black Man:

Black Man   Ongiini.

Actor 6   A Herero tribesman,

Actors 1, 3, 4, 5   The He-re-ro.

Actor 6   Keeping watch over his cattle as they graze.
As he has done his entire life,
And as his father did before him,
And as his grandfather before him,
And as his great-grandfather before him.
Let's see if he will speak with us:
Ongiini, Herero Man.

Black Man   Ongiini.

Actor 6   Wonderful, he is feeling sociable.
Herero Man, please tell us about yourself.

Black Man   I am a Herero man.
I am a herdsman.

Actor 6   Are cattle very valuable to you?

Black Man   Why yes, yes they are.
Traditionally, the Herero find value in cattle, in land and
in fire.

Actor 6   In fire?

Black Man   Yes, fire.

Actor 6   How interesting. Tell us more.

Black Man   Each Herero family has a fire in their backyard.
The Herero believe that this fire contains the souls of their
ancestors.
Because of this, they believe that the fire must be kept
constantly burning or else their ancestors will be destroyed.

Actor 6   Thank you for sharing your traditional belief
system with us.
And look!
A second Herero Man is approaching.
Our German soldier –

White Man   Guten Tag.

Actor 6   Watches them interact.

Another Black Man   Ongiini.

Black Man   Ongiini.

White Man   They greet each other.

Sarah *moos as cow.*

Another Black Man   What a beautiful cow.

White Man   A compliment.

Actor 6   Our German soldier documents his discovery in a
letter to Sarah:

Sarah   Ach! Liebe!

White Man   Dear Sarah.
I continue to be impressed by the members of one tribe in
particular: the Herero.

Not only are they tall and well muscled,
They are more sociable and sweet tempered than I had
expected –

Scene: Process

Actor 5   Stop. Ok? Just stop.

Actor 1   What?

Actor 5 *is having a full-on freak-out.*

Actor 5   I don't know what I'm doing.

Actor 6   You're doing great –

Actor 5   But I don't know who I am supposed to be. Or
what I'm allowed to –

Actor 6   It's fine. Let's just go back to the letter, and just be
yourself, in the moment –

Actor 5   NO. Listen to me. *I don't know what my character is
doing.*

Actor 6   Ok.

Actor 5   I don't know what my perspective is to what's
happening,
I don't know what my motivation is,
I don't know what my active verb is,
I don't know what my spine is shaped like,
I don't know what my – my me means –

Actor 6   Ok. Ok. Sarah.

Actor 5   My name is *not* Sarah.

Actor 6   Yes it is –

Actor 5   No it's not.

Actor 6   Your name is Sarah / and you are a German
woman –

Actor 5   But I'm not. And I don't know how to do this right.

Actor 6   Listen to me –

Actor 5   Everything I say is somehow wrong,

Actor 6   That's not true.

Actor 5   Like I'm not allowed to say anything or do anything, and I don't even know what I'm trying to do –

Actor 4   You're telling the story of the Herero genocide. Ok?

Actor 5   But I'm –

Actor 4   You're trying. Alright?
Now listen to me.
Your name is Sarah. You are a German woman.

Actor 5   I don't know how to do this.

Actor 4   Just listen to me and explore. Ok?

Actor 5   Ok.

Actor 4 (*painting the picture for her*)   You grew up someplace remote. Like . . . Zwickau.
And you moved South, to München,
And saw the Rhine for the first time,
And the new people
And new strassen
And new streudelschnecken
All so exciting.
But still, you missed your parents, your family, your home.

Actor 6   Great.

Actor 4   Now who are you?

Actor 5   I am Sarah.

Actor 4   Right.

Actor 6   Well, hello Sarah.

Actor 5/Sarah   Hello.

Actor 6   Pleased to meet you, Sarah.

Actor 5/Sarah   I am pleased to meet you. Pleased as punch.

Actor 6   What a delightful expression, Sarah.

Actor 5/Sarah   I say it all the time.

Actor 6   Who do you say it to, Sarah?

Actor 5/Sarah   I say pleased as punch to my children.

Actor 6   Oh, I don't think Sarah has children / maybe she's a teacher, or –

Actor 5/Sarah	**Actor 4**
She has two boys.	[Let her do it.]
Two blond little men.	

Actor 6   Sarah.

Actor 5/Sarah   There is Heiner. And
Leipzig.

Actor 5 *adopts a 'German' accent. It's not ok.*
Actor 4 *might begin to hum Edelweiss.*

Sarah   Ach! Leipzig! Liebe Leipzig!
Ze boyz at school are zo mean to mein liebe Leipzig
Until ein tag, I take Leipzig by the shoulders:

She grabs **Actor 4**.

Sarah   und I look him in ze eyes
und I say to him,
Leipzig,
look at me Leipzig!

Actor 4 *becomes Leipzig, with 'German' accent.*

Actor 4 (*as Leipzig*)   Ach! Mama! Ze boyz!

Sarah   I know, Leipzig.
You listen to Mama.
Find ze grossest boy und give him ein shtomp:

Actor 4 (*as Leipzig*)   Shtomp!

Sarah   Und ein drang:

Actor 4 (*as Leipzig*)   Drang!

Sarah   Und the next day, at kindergarten –

Actor 6   Sarah.

Sarah   – Leipzig valked up to ze grossest boy,

Actor 4 *walks over to* **Actor 3**.

Actor 4 (*as Leipzig*)   Hallo, Boy.

Actor 3 (*as Grossest Boy*)   Hallo, Leipzig.

Sarah   Und shtomp!

Actor 4 '*shtomps*' **Actor 3**.

Actor 3 (*as Grossest Boy*)   Ach!

Sarah   Und drang!

Actor 4 '*drangs*' **Actor 3**.

Actor 3 (*as Grossest Boy*)   Ach!

Sarah   Und ze boy cried for heez muter.

Actor 3 (*as Grossest Boy*)   Mama!

Sarah   Und Leipzig lift happily eva afta.

Sarah and Actor 4   Yay!

Actor 6   Guys.

Sarah (*with a smile*)   Da?

Actor 6   We've established that Sarah doesn't have children yet.

Actor 5/Sarah   I have decided that I have my Leipzig.

Actor 6   But you can't.

Actor 4 (*as Leipzig being dragged away*)   Mama!

Actor 5   What if only I know?

Actor 1   The letters we're reading talk about wanting a family, not having one.

Actor 5/Sarah   He is your son too.

Actor 6   You can be Sarah without him.

Actor 5/Sarah   I want my Leipzig.

Actor 1   But –

Actor 3   Maybe you *have* lost children.

Actor 5/Sarah   Liebe Leipzig.

Actor 6   No –

Actor 3   Maybe she's lost children.

Actor 6   But –

Actor 3   And they're dead,

Actor 5/Sarah (*a gasp*).

Actor 3   And you're longing for your husband to come back, across the ocean, and make more children.

Actor 6   I don't think –

Actor 5   Across the sea.

Actor 3 (*to* **Actor 6**)   The stakes are so high.

Actor 5/Sarah   My husband.

Actor 3   Right?

Actor 5   Yeah.

Actor 3   Not just your husband your – your 'future family'.

Actor 5/Sarah   My future.

Actor 3   Right.

Actor 6   Ok.

Actor 5/Sarah   All Sarah wants is to be impregnated.

Actor 6   Um.

Actor 3   Yes.

Actor 6   Alright.

Scene: Presentation [1888]

Sarah *begins to sing a melodramatic folk song with total
commitment and sincerity.
It sounds kind of like Edelweiss.*

Sarah   To the north, across the sea,
I sit and wait, wait for thee,
Distant husband. Where is he?
I sit and wait, wait for thee.

*A beat is introduced, and complicated. The song becomes the dance
re-mix of itself.*

With my womb, lying empty,
Like my heart. Come back to me,
My husband. I wait for thee.
I wait for our family.

*And then they break it down.
It's pretty awesome.
The actors might spit beats,
and sample a popular song or two.
Aww, yeah.
Out of this,*
White Man *kind of raps a letter.*
Black Man *beat boxes or hypes him or something.*

White Man   Dear Sarah.
I have never been in a hotter place in my whole life.
The whole place, as far as I can tell is a desert.
I know there is ocean to the west, but I have never seen it.
All everyone talks about is rain.

Wondering if it will rain, when it will rain, how much it
will rain,
This passes for sport in these parts.
There are trees of course, and those with the best shade
are hotly contested for.
There is one tree, the best without a doubt,
With shade that is, inexplicably, 5 full degrees cooler than
the shade of any other tree.
I have named this tree
Sarah.

Scene: Process

A shift. Everything is probably less awesome.

Actor 6   Keep going.

Actor 1   That's the end of the letter.

Actor 6   You're doing so well, just stay with it.
Explore.
Go back to the end of the letter, and give us some more.

Uh-oh.
Beat boxing, sort of.

Actor 1   I have named this tree Sarah.
Because that is your name.
And I like you – I love you –
Like I love . . . / trees?

Actor 6   No no we don't need more
we need deeper.
We need to see more of this world, we need / to see more –

Actor 3   We need to set the scene.
It's like, where is he? He's writing this letter but
Where is he?
What else is happening?
Who is he *with*?
What are *we doing* while he is writing the letter.

Actor 6   You're right.

Actor 3   I know.
So, we're soldiers, we've spent all day doing like colonial
soldier-y stuff and
we're tired and
we've come back to our –
our bivouac –

Actor 1   Our what?

Actor 3   Our, like, rustic military tent camp thing.

Actor 1   Got it.

Actor 3   And it's been a long day, and we get back to the
bivouac and we're –
Building a fire.

Actor 6   Try it.

The worst improv ever.
Actor 1 *and* **Actor 3** *build a fire.*
They light the fire.
They take turns blowing at the fire.
The fire catches.
Actor 1 *is not a great improv partner.*

Actor 3   Do you know when he'll get here?

Actor 1   Who?

Actor 3   The General.

Actor 1   Oh – I don't know.

Actor 3   I thought you said you knew.

Actor 1   But I don't.

This isn't working. Can we stop?

Actor 6   Keep going.

Actor 3   Are you hungry?

Actor 1   Are you hungry?

Actor 3   I could eat something down to the bone.
And you. You must be starving.

Actor 1   I don't know maybe I am, maybe I'm not. This
isn't helping.

Actor 3   Ok, so what are we doing by the fire?

Actor 1   Well, I'm . . . trying to write a letter.

Actor 3   Yeah.

Actor 1   So I should just write the letter.

Actor 3   But that's not –
Ok. Just tell me:
What do you think of the General?

Actor 1   I don't know.

Actor 3   I think the General is a fine man. Don't you think
so?
That's something we soldiers would talk about, round
the fire.

Actor 1   Sure.

Actor 3   Ah, the General.
The General – is the reason I joined up.
As a boy growing up in *Cologne*,
I knew that I was meant for greater things – to see the
world.
And that starts here.
This is my first assignment.
Is this your first assignment?

Actor 1   I'm just trying to write this letter.

Actor 3   Yeah.
Who is the letter to?

Actor 1   Sarah.

Actor 3   Good. Why are you writing it?

Actor 1   Why don't I just read it?

Actor 3   No.

Actor 1   Why not?

Actor 3   Well, because I don't think a soldier would share his personal letter with another soldier.

Actor 1   But, I don't mind.

Actor 3   Go ahead.

Scene: Presentation [1896]

White Man *and* **Sarah** *are dominant in the presentation.*
The letter is filled with romance and yearning.
There might be some distant representation of African bodies . . . but the love is foregrounded.

White Man   Dear Sarah.
We awoke before dawn again this morning.
And walked, and walked,
And walked until long after dark.
We walk so much even when I sleep
I dream of walking in the heat.
There is so much heat here, Sarah.

I saw steam rising from the shoulders of the man in front of me.
It is so hot our very sweat is wrested from our bodies.
I have never experienced such thirst as this.
Dear Sarah, I beg you
for a picture, of you in our garden,
for a picture of you in a cool and living place.
I will hold your picture to my lips and feel refreshed.

Scene: Process

Actor 4   Can I ask a question?

Actor 6   What is it?

Actor 2   Are we just going to sit here and watch some white people fall in love all day?

Actor 4   I wasn't going to put it like that –

Actor 2   Where are all the Africans?

Actor 1   We're just reading the letters.
I'm sure we'll find something that has some more context.

Actor 2   I think we should see some Africans in Africa.

Actor 1   And I think we have to stick with what we have
access to.

Actor 2   No no no. This is some
Out-of-Africa-African-Queen-bullshit you all are pulling
right here, ok?
If we are in Africa, I want to see some black people.

Actor 6   He's right. We have to see more of the Herero.

Actor 4   That's all I was trying to say.

Actor 6   We need to see what –

Actor 4   We need to see Africa.

Actor 2   That's what I'm talking about.

Actor 4   You know? These dusty old letters talking about
this dusty old place –

Actor 2   Yes.

Actor 4   I want to see the live Africa.

Actor 2   Preach.

Actor 4   The Africa that's lush –

Actor 2   Um –

Actor 4   The Africa that's green

Actor 2   Well –

Actor 4   With fruit dripping from trees –

Actor 6   Dig into it.

Actor 2   But the desert –

Actor 4   Gold pushing its way out of the ground –

Actor 2   That's not –

Actor 6 (*to* **Actor 2**)   Shh –

Actor 4   And so many animals –

Actor 6   Yes.

Actor 4   Monkeys –

Actor 6   Yes.

Actor 4   Gibbons –

Actor 6   Yes.

Actor 4   Elephants and giant snakes –

Actor 6   Stick with it.

Actor 4/Another Black Man   And I hunt them.

Actor 4 *adopts an 'African' accent. It's not ok.*

Another Black Man   I hunt de lion. I hunt de jagua. I hunt de tiegah.

Actor 2   But –

Actors 3, 5, 6   Shhh.

Another Black Man   When I kill a tiegah I eat de heart of the animal while it beats.

'African' drums begin, slowly, provided by **Actor 6**.
The beat is felt in a count of 7
(1–2, 1–2, 1–2-3).

Another Black Man   I push my hands inside the animal,
breaking apart bone and sinew, until I reach the heart
and I pull it towards my heart, feeling
the veins stretch and snap, wiping
spurts of blood from my face.

By now, **Actors 1**, **3** *and* **5**, *have found the beat also.*
Now it starts to grow.

Another Black Man   I barely have to chew, the heart is
tender.
I pull a fang from the animal's mouth and add it to my
necklace of teeth –
another kill,
another point of pride,
another day I provide for my family.
My family – we feast on the best parts of the meat,
we feast, and women ululate

Actor 5 *ululates.*

Another Black Man   and dance with naked breasts

Actor 5 *performs 'African' dance. Others join.*

Another Black Man   in front of our fire.
And they are all my wives, the women are all my wives
and I take two of them to my bed,
and I fuck both of the wives I took to bed
and I make them both pregnant because we are all as dark
and fertile as African jungle soil.

'African' dance and drumming and joy.

Actor 2 *breaks in:*

Actor 2   You all need to stop.

Another Black Man   I have many children. Many many
children.

Actor 2   For real. Just stop.

Actor 5   Keep going!

Another Black Man   Many children that I love.

Actor 2   STOP.

They stop.

Actor 2   This isn't that kind of Africa.
Ok?
We already Wikipediaed this.

Actor 5   Yeah, but –

Actor 2   We know it's like desert: dry, hot, arid, barren.
What's he talking about tigers and palm trees –

Actor 4   I was making the part my own.

Actor 2   Oh come on.

Actor 5   You don't want us to do anything.

Actor 2   You can't make the part your own so much that
you ignore what's actually there.

Actor 1   That's not what he's saying.

Actor 2   Oh really?

Actor 1   It's not.

Actor 2   So why don't you tell me what he's saying.

Actor 5   Why are you always so angry all the time?

Actor 2   I know you didn't.

Actor 5   What?

Actor 4   Guys I know that I don't know everything about
the Herero but –
Will you listen? We have to start somewhere.

Actor 2   So start by being black.

Beat.

Actor 6   Ok guys.

Actor 4   What are you trying to say?

Actor 2   I'm just saying that –

Actor 6   Ok.

Actor 2   That black people should know – Ok.
(*Being more careful with his words than before.*)
Black people can understand what black people went
through.

Actor 4   So basically, you're saying that I'm not [black] –

Actor 2   All I'm saying is we all should be thinking about
being black right now.

Actor 6   Ok, guys,

Actor 5   What he means is –

Actor 6   What he's saying is that the whole point of this
whole thing is that
these people aren't so different from us.
Right? Right.
Like, for me the whole idea for this whole presentation
started when I sat down
in my house, in my kitchen
and I opened a magazine
and I saw my grandmother's face
in the middle of a page.
So I read the story around her face,
and the story was about people I'd never heard of,
in a place I'd never cared about.
An entire tribe of people nearly destroyed.
People who looked like my family.
And I thought about *my family*.
My father.
My grandmother –
a woman who died before I was born.
And I've missed her my whole life, and I always
wondered what she would have sounded like,
and here she was,
speaking to me through the picture of this Herero
woman. *That* was my way in.
It was like I was having a conversation with my
grandmother.

Actor 5 *becomes Grandma. It's not ok.*

Actor 5   Ooooh, chil'.

Actor 6   What are you –

Actor 5   Come on guys! Let's improv it!

Actor 2   Oh hell no.

Actor 4   Awesome.

Actor 6   Oh, I don't think we need to.

Actor 4   We should at least try it.

Actor 6   I don't think so.

Actor 5   Why not?

Actor 3   Because she wouldn't be in charge.

Actor 6   I'm not –

Actor 3   It's not supposed to be about leading or following.

Actor 4 (*sung*)   We're all in this together.

Actor 6   I'm just trying to tell you that –

Actor 5 (*as Grandma*) Whatchu think this is? Weez in it now. Can't just tell a talk no mo.

Actor 4   Come on, we'll support you. Just talk to her.

Actor 5 (*as Grandma*)   Talk to me girl.

Actor 2   Mmn-mm, we aren't doing this.

Actor 6   No. No – we can do this. But this is my grandma, ok? I can't just –

Actor 4 *becomes Grandma. Again, not ok.*

Actor 4 (*as Grandma*)   Ooooh, chil'. Talk to me, girl.

Actor 6   Uh-uh. We are exploring, but that is just too Tyler Perry for me.

Actor 3 *becomes Grandma. Not ok.*
But . . . pretty good?

Actor 3 (*as Grandma*)   Ooooh, chil'.

Actor 6   Oh no –

Actor 3   Mmmmmmm-hmm. You can't play your own grandma, girl.

Actor 6   You're right, but my grandma –

Actor 3 (*as Grandma*)   Don't 'My grandma' me. You better let me talk when I am talking, girl.
There's talking and then there's listening
and when I'm around
you better just introduce yourself as listening.

Beat. **Actor 5** *jumps and claps.*

Actor 5   Yay!

Actor 6   Ok. Fine.

Actor 3 (*as Grandma*)   Right.

Actor 6   So, my grandma was full of folksy expressions, according to my dad.
My dad would say–

Actor 4 *becomes Dad.*

Actor 4 (*as Dad*)   My mother had more folk in her than Glastonbury.

Actor 6   Well –

Actor 2   That's not how black people talk.

Actor 4   That's how my dad talked.

Actor 2   Black people don't make jokes about Glastonbury.

Actor 6 (*pulling* **Actor 4** *back into the improv*)   My dad talked about my grandma's bulla cake.

Actor 3 (*in Grandma voice, to other* **Actors**)   Now, somebody better get me something to cook with. Grandma needs a prop.

Actor 6 (*trying to get back to her story*)   Ok guys –

Actor 3 (*to* **Actor 4** *as Dad, creating a scene*)   You touch that bulla cake again, you'll be pulling back a stump, you hear me?

Actor 4 (*as Dad*)   Yeah.

Actor 3 (*as Grandma*)   Don't yeah me.

Actor 3 *hits* **Actor 4**.

Actor 4 (*as Dad*)   Ow! Yes, mama.

Actor 6   That's interesting, because you couldn't sass my grandma –

Actor 3 *hits* **Actor 4**.

Actor 4 (*as Dad*)   Ow!

Actor 3 (*as Grandma*)   Don't sass me boy.

Actor 4 (*as Dad*)   Yes, Mama.

Actor 3 *smacks* **Actor 4** *with his prop on each 'Tell'*.

Actor 3 (*as Grandma*)   Tell me that you didn't eat that bulla cake.
Tell me that you didn't hear me say don't you eat that bulla cake.
Tell me that you didn't come in here, after I told you not to, and eat that bulla cake.

Actor 6   So –

Actor 3 (*as Grandma*)   Tell me that corner piece isn't missing.

Actor 6   Ok –

Actor 3 (*as Grandma*)   Tell me that you didn't eat that corner piece of bulla cake.
I don't need you to Tell me that you ate that corner piece of bulla cake.
I can Tell the corner is missing so Tell me that you ate it.
Tell me.
Tell me.

Actor 6   He ate the bulla cake.

Actor 3 (*as Grandma*)   I know he ate the bulla cake.

Actor 6   Now, my dad doesn't eat bulla cake –

Actor 3 (*as Grandma*)   Not any more you don't.

Actor 6   – because of my grandmother.
Who I never met.

Actor 3 (*as Grandma*)   I'm standin' right here, girl.

Actor 6   Do you see what I'm saying, people?
The woman in that article looked just like my grandmother
and that doesn't happen to me –
I don't belong to a tribe
I don't know where my ancestors were from
I don't have a homeland where people look like me
I'm just British, Black British, and
people tell me I look like other women all the time
but I never actually look like these other women they sayI
look like
not really
because to some people
all black women look the same.

But the woman in this article.
She looked like my grandmother.
And suddenly I felt like I have a lineage.
I felt like maybe
I could point to a place
a specific country
a specific homeland
and I could say
there.
My family is from there.
And I found that because my grandmother came to me
and told me about a genocide, where eight out of every
ten people in this tribe
my tribe had been murdered.

Actor 3 (*as Grandma*)   It's terrible what those people do to each other.

Actor 6   My grandma wouldn't have said that.

Actor 3 (*as Grandma*)   You ain't ever met me, girl.

Actor 6   She wouldn't say that.

Actor 3 (*as Grandma*)   You don't even know who I am.

Actor 6   I know it wasn't really my grandmother in that picture.
But the woman in that picture could have been my grandma.

Actor 3 (*as Grandma*)   Have you gone crazy?
You can't be somebody when you're already somebody.

Actor 6   But if things had been different –

Actor 3 (*as Grandma*)   Then you would be different.

Actor 6   I know, but, just –

Actor 3 (*as Grandma*)   Just what?

Actor 6   Just taking a walk in someone else's shoes –

Actor 3 (*as Grandma*)   Ain't no puttin' on nobody else's shoes / and walkin' around –

Actor 6   Alright, that's enough.

Actor 3 (*as Grandma*)   – sayin' this is this and that is that –

Actor 6   I said that's enough.

Actor 3 (*as Grandma*)   You better shut your mouth and listen to me, girl.
You can't take no walk in somebody else's shoes and know anything.
You ain't bought those shoes,
you ain't laced those shoes up,
you ain't put those shoes on day after day,
you ain't broken those shoes in.
Now, you can borrow somebody else's shoes, and
you can walk as long as you want,

they ain't your shoes.
You can go ahead and steal somebody else's shoes and
guess what?
They ain't your shoes.

Scene: Presentation [1898]

White Man   Dear Sarah.
My shoes have finally worn completely through,
from all of our walking along the rails.
Sturdy old things,
they lasted far longer than they should have, I'm sure.

He destroys this letter.
He begins again.

Dear Sarah.
We have come across some problems
building this railroad into the interior.
For one thing, it has been extremely dry –
tens, if not dozens, of natives drop off
each and every day.
I fear for their morale,
and for, in turn, our safety.

He destroys this letter.
He begins again.

Dear Sarah.
The railroad has been a great success.
The satisfaction in setting sturdy steel in straight lines
towards the horizon,
Civilizing this wild landscape – it is a testament to German –

He destroys this letter.
He makes up a letter he doesn't write
and would never send – a true letter.

Dear Sarah.
I've been meaning to thank you for your letters.
I would like to put each note
Back in its envelope,
Stack them in a stack
On my tongue and swallow the
Whole stack whole.

He destroys this letter –
The true letter.
He writes the real letter.

Dear Sarah.
The weather has been more temperate of late.
But it has been dry here, Sarah.
For all our sakes, I hope that soon it will
Rain.

Scene: Process

Actor 2   Dear Sarah, Let me tell you some boring shit.

Actor 6   Come on –

Actor 2   Dear Sarah, You thought that last shit was boring?
Well, you won't even believe how boring this new shit's
gonna be.

Actor 6   Alright –

Actor 2   Dear Sarah, I'm killing black people every single
day
but I'm not going to tell you about that
not when I can talk some more boring shit about your
garden or your tree
to your boring skinny arse.

Actor 5   That's not fair –

Actor 2   You said we would get some Africa in here.

Actor 6   I know.

Actor 3   You know, I think –

Actor 2   And we're just reading these stupid letters.
We're never going to find out anything about the Africans
in these letters.
Sarah doesn't care about black people.

Actor 3   Alright, Kanye.

Actor 2   You think that's nice innit?

Actor 6   Hold it hold it hold it.
You're right. You are. We need to see more of the Herero.
We do.
And you know what? The letters aren't enough.

Actor 5   But they're so important.

Actor 6   I'm not saying they aren't important, but they
aren't enough.

Actor 5   But –

Actor 1   So what do you want us to do?

Actor 6   I want us –

Actor 1   We can't just improvise the whole thing.

Actor 2	**Actor 6**
Why not?	I'm not saying that –

Because he's afraid of improv?

Actor 1   I'm not afraid of improv.

Actor 3   You're kind of afraid of improv.

Actor 1   We shouldn't be pretending, we shouldn't be
making things up, we shouldn't be doing anything other
than what's real.

Actor 6   I am agreeing with you –

Actor 2   What's real is that they don't even talk about
Africans in those letters.

Actor 1   But these letters are the only thing we actually
know.

Actor 6   That's not true –

Actor 1   They're the only personal, first-person stories we have.

Actor 6   That is actually not the truth.

Actor 2   The letters don't have any evidence of anything happening to the Africans. They don't mention one prison camp, one hanging, one incident of –

Actor 1   So how do we know what even happened to them? We –

Actor 2	**Actor 4**
So you're saying that we just Made up the genocide?	What do you mean how do we know?

Actor 1   I'm not saying the genocide was made up. I'm just saying we don't have physical evidence –

Actor 6   So where do you think all the people went?

Actor 1   I'm not saying it didn't happen –

Actor 4   Because we know that it happened.

Actor 6   We've done research –

Actor 3   But we haven't found anything about / the Herero.

Actor 2   We did all kinds of searches –

Actor 1   Yeah, on the internet.

Actor 6   Yes –

Actor 1   But these letters are the only *physical* evidence of –

Actor 5   He's just saying that it's not like the Holocaust.

Beat.

Actor 6   What?

Actor 5   No I don't mean – I just mean –

Actor 4   It is exactly like that.

Actor 5   I don't mean it like that – it's just like we know exactly what happened during the – that because of all the evidence.

Actor 4   So you're saying –

Actor 1   Right, she's saying –

Actor 5   I'm just saying we don't have the same kind of evidence for this. That's all.
You know? We just have the letters.

Actor 1   Exactly.

Actor 2   But we know –

Actor 1   With the Holocaust, we have documents, we have testimonials, we have pictures.

Actor 6   There are pictures of the Herero –

Actor 1   But not –

Actor 6   I showed you all the picture of that woman,

Actor 1   I know –

Actor 6   That old woman, who had been forced out into the desert, and barely made it, she was starved half to death, and she looked exactly like those pictures from –

Actor 1   But we don't know who she is. We have no idea who she is.

Actor 3   We don't even know her name.

Actor 1   Six million people
and we know all of their names.
Every single one.
And –

Actor 4   We don't know the Herero names.

Actor 1   Exactly –

Actor 4   But that doesn't mean they weren't murdered.

Actor 1   That's not what I'm saying –

Actor 4   It's not like –

Actor 6   It's not like you can compare –

Actor 4   It's not like, oh, a tree falls in a forest, does it make a sound.
The tree fell. We know it fell.

Actor 6   It's –

Actor 4   It hasn't made a sound, it's not going to make a sound because it already fell.

Actor 5   I see what you're saying, but –

Actor 4   So what if we don't know their names. So what if we don't know exactly.

Actor 5   But –

Actor 4   We know enough.

Actor 5   Enough to *what*, though?

Actor 6   We know that it happened.

Actor 1   We are telling this story. This letter says –

Actor 6   We all keep saying the letter says, the letter says, But we don't need to follow exactly what the letters say.

Actor 1   So then what are we going to do.

Actor 6   I want you to make a letter up. [We need to clear the space, people.]

Actor 1   Well I don't feel comfortable doing that.

Actor 6   I don't want you to feel comfortable. I want you to do it.

Actor 1   But it's –

Actor 6   What?

Actor 1   It's history, there's facts, there's truth. I have no idea what it's really like to be someone like him. And I'm trying to figure out what kind of – who does something like – how someone can –

Actor 6   So just be yourself, in his situation.

Actor 1   But I'm nothing like him.

Actor 6   You don't know that.

Actor 1   Yes I do.

Actor 5   Just talk to me.

Actor 6   All we're talking about is writing a letter home.

Actor 5   I'll support you.

Actor 1   Fine.

Actor 5   Great.

Actor 2   This is just going to be more white letters.

Actor 6   No, because I want you to own the letter he's writing.

Actor 2   What does that mean?

Actor 6   I just want to start with this, to build –

Actor 2   Start what?

Actor 6   Just to use his words to –

Actor 2   I have my own words.

Actor 6   I need you to trust me, Ok? Please.

Actor 2   Ok.

Actor 5   He needs a wife.

Actor 6   We're just developing –

Actor 5   He does.

Actor 3   She's right. If we're doing the whole love thing.

Actor 6   Fine, I'll do it.

Actor 3   But –

Actor 6   We're creating the Herero story, and for now, I'll
be the Herero woman, the black woman, whatever.
Let's stop talking about it and just try it. Ok?

Actor 5   Ok.

Actor 6   And, the letter is just a starting point, ok, people?
We all know that this ends in a genocide, so let's get there.
White Man, start us off.

Scene: Presentation [1899]

At the start, **White Man** *and* **Sarah** *are foregrounded.*

Black Man   *builds a fire.*

White Man   Dear Sarah.
I am hungry enough to eat something down to the bone.
As I write this I can hear you laugh –

Sarah *and* **Black Woman** *laugh.*

White Man   – and say –

Sarah   You are always hungry.

White Man   And I know it to be true.
The smell of meat over fire reminds me –

During the following . . .

Sarah   Reminds me of the time we ate off sticks round the
fire. When we ate our sausages off sticks and hoped that
they'd cooked all the way through.

Black Man *and* **Black Woman** *warm themselves by the fire.*

White Man   Reminds me of you –

Sarah   Until it began to rain –

Black Man *and* **Black Woman** *look up at the rain.*

White Man   It's raining here.
That reminds me –

Sarah   – until it began to rain and we had to duck in under
that one tree in the field, in our field, and you told me we'd
be struck by lightning –

Black Man *runs under the tree.*

Black Woman *is beautiful, enjoying the rain.*

Sarah   – I wanted to run away from that tree as fast as
I could but
I wanted to stay as dry as I could and as warm as I could
so I ended up doing neither.

White Man   The rain reminds me of you too.

Black Man   Dear Sarah.

White Man   Dear Sarah.

Black Man   Dear, dear, Sarah.

White Man   Do you remember when it rained?

Black Woman   I love the rain.

White Man   We huddled under the tree.

Black Man   You're shivering.

Black Woman   I'm warm enough.

Sarah   Trying to keep warm.

Black Man   I could keep you warmer.

White Man   You looked so good wet
I told you if we stayed under the tree you'd get electrocuted.

Black Man   You better come back under here.

White Man   It might have been true.

Black Woman   It's only water.

Black Man   Look at you –

Black Woman   How do I look?

White Man   We ran out into the rain, and back under the tree –

Black Man   Give me your hands.

Black Woman   Are you afraid of the rain?

White Man   – and out into the rain, and back under the tree –

Black Man   I'm not afraid of anything.

White Man   You were soaked –

Sarah   Soaked down to the bone, my fingernails —

Black Man   Your fingernails are blue.

Sarah   The tips were clear like I'd been in a bath.

White Man   And I held your hands and made them warm.

Black Man   Come here and let me warm you up.

Black Woman   Thank you.

Black Man   Look at you. Soaked right down to the hair on your arms.

Black Woman   I don't have hairy arms.

Black Man   That's a shame. Since I like it so much.

Black Woman   Really.

Black Man   Oh Sarah, the hair on your arms.

Black Woman   What about it?

Black Man   I could write letters and letters about your arms.
Dear Sarah.
Do you remember the water, when we could go west to
the ocean?
And the rain –
do you remember swimming in the water while it rained?

Before the lightning struck?
We got out just before the lightning struck –
The sky and water were grey.
Your hair smells dirty when it's wet
and I told you so and you cried
and lightning struck the water
and the wet hair on our arms stood up.
And someday we will say
do you remember that tree? When it rained?
When we leaned in close to the trunk?
And there was lightning
and thunder
and Sarah under that tree.
The hair on your arms slicked down.
Dear Sarah.
I think you should be my wife.
I think we should have children.
What do you think about that?

Black Woman   All you have to do is ask.

Black Man   Will you be my wife?

Black Woman   Yes.

Black Man   Will you have my children?

Black Woman   Yes.

Black Man   You are my family.

They kiss.

Scene: Process

Actor 2 *is kissing* **Actor 6**. *She stops kissing him. He doesn't stop kissing her. She struggles to get away. She starts arranging things, moving things.*

Actor 2   What are you doing?

Actor 6   We're moving on.

Actor 3   Ok. What are we doing?

Actor 6   We need to do more Herero stuff, right?

Actor 4   Like a village?

Actor 6   Yes.

Actor 3   So we're just going to set one up?

Actor 6   Yes.

Actor 2   Do you have a better idea?

Actor 3   I have like seven better ideas.

Actor 4   Let's just try this, ok?

Actor 3   Let's just set up a village.

Actor 4   Yes.

Actor 3   I'm an actor not a stagehand.

Actor 4   Oh my God.

Actor 2   Why are you even here?

Actor 3   Me?

Actor 2   You clearly don't want to tell this story.

Actor 3   I've been trying to make this a poignant –

Actor 2   Mmh-hhmn.

Actor 3   – and professional from the very beginning.

Actor 6   Guys.

Actor 3   You're the one that keeps stopping everything.

Actor 2   Because you all keep trying to pull some stupid shit.

Actor 3   If you think it's all so stupid, why don't you just leave?

Actor 6   No.

Actor 2   You'd like that wouldn't you.

Actor 6   Guys –

Actor 3   Yes, actually I think we all would.

Actor 6   No.

Actor 2   And leave you all to try and put this thing together?

Actor 3   I think we would be fine without –

Actor 2   Uh-uh, no way, what this thing needs is someone that is thinking about the black experience.

Actor 3   Oh please.

Actor 4   We're all thinking about that.

Actor 2   You need me here.

Actor 6   Guys. I'm not saying this again.
No one is leaving, ok?
We all said we wanted to do this.
All I want to do is tell this story.

Actor 2   So do I.

Actor 4   So do I.

Actor 5   So let's just do it.
What are we doing? Making the village.

Actor 6   Yes.

Actor 5   Ok.
We have huts over here.
And like the sacred fire –

Actor 4   Is right here.

Actor 5   Perfect.

Actor 6   Great.

Actor 4   And . . .

Actor 5   And there's cows, and the men watching cows. (*To* **Actor 2** *and* **Actor 4**.) You guys watch cows, ok? Please? (*To* **Actor 1** *and* **Actor 3**.) And you guys watch them watch the cows. (*To* **Actor 6**.) And whatever, we're here. We're like –

Actor 5 *wraps something around her head – a scarf, a sweater.*

Actor 5   The wives. We can be making a fire, or –

Actor 2   This is exactly what I'm talking about.

Actor 5   We can make a cooking fire –

Actor 2 (*to* **Actor 6**)   How can you stand there and let her do that?

Actor 6   I'm not –

Actor 1   Just let her make the stupid fire.

Actor 2 (*to* **Actor 5**)   You aren't a Herero wife, ok?

Actor 1   She can be whatever she wants.

Actor 5   We're finding the Herero in us.

Actor 2   No, we're finding the Herero in *us* –

Actor 6   We're all trying to find the Herero –

Actor 2   You lot are finding Germans in you.

Actor 5   Well, I don't only want to be a German.

Actor 2   Too bad.

Actor 5   I want to have another part.

Actor 2   Well, you can't be an African.

Actor 5   I think I can –

Actor 2   You can't / it doesn't make any sense.

Actor 5   I just need / to get into my body.

Actor 4   What if you were a German sometimes?

Actor 2   That wouldn't make any sense either.

Actor 3   He couldn't play a German.

Actor 2   Oh, I could play a German.

Actor 6   Guys.

Actor 2   If we were doing some stupid-ass thing like that
I would be a better German than you / because I
understand it
because I've been to Germany.

Actor 3   Oh, you think so, do you?

Actor 1 (*response to* **Actor 2**'s '*I've been to Germany*')   Oh, here
we go.

Actor 2   What, I can't go to Germany?

Actor 6   That's not what he's –

Actor 2   I've been to Germany.

Actor 6   Ok.

Actor 2   I love Germany. I love German people.
And you know what?

Actor 6   Ok.

Actor 2   I was very successful in Germany, ok? You know
what I'm saying?

He's saying that he had a lot of sex.

Actor 6   Ok, guys.

Actor 2   That's not even bragging that's just the truth.

Actor 1   Well, have you ever been to Africa?

Actor 2   Have you ever been to Africa?

Actor 1   I'm not trying to play an African.

Actor 2   No you're not. Because you can't.

Actor 1   You know what?

Actor 2   What.

Actor 6   Guys.

Actor 1   I have had just about enough of your flipping attitude.

Actor 2   Of my attitude?

Actor 1   First you're yelling at him for not getting it right, not being African right.

Actor 2   I'm not yelling at anybody.

Actor 6   Nobody's –

Actor 1   You're yelling at her, you're yelling at me, but you don't know anymore than any of us.

Actor 6   We're –

Actor 1   None of us has ever been to Africa.

Actor 2   Yeah, and I don't need to go to Africa to know what it's like to be black.

Actor 1   You're not supposed to be black, you're supposed to be African.

Actor 2   There's no difference between being black and being African / Africa is black.

Actor 1   Of course there is a difference. That is ridiculous.

Actor 2   You better get out of my face.

Actor 1   You don't know the difference between being black and being African?

Actor 2   I said you better get out of my face.

Actor 6   Guys guys guys.
Break it up.

She separates the men.

Actor 5   Maybe we should take a break.

Actor 6   No. No more breaks, no more letters, no more bullshit, I've had enough.
You boys need to check your egos and put it into the work.
Ok?

Actor 2   That's fine with me.

Actor 6   I said enough.
Sarah, when are we?

Actor 5   Um . . .

Actor 6   Where are we?

Actor 5   I don't know.

Actor 6   Oh come on.

Actor 5   We might have to go back a little.

Actor 6   To what?

Actor 5   To . . . 1892.

Actor 6   Are you serious?

Actor 5   We haven't built the railroad, we haven't / changed the laws, we haven't executed anyone –

Actor 6   Ok I get it ok.
We need to get it together people.
Let's go. 1892.

Actor 5   It's the Germans training the Herero and giving them the cows part.

Actor 6   So let's start training. Right now. Let's go people.

Actor 5   We should be like marching?

She marches.

Actor 6   Yes. Hup two three four.
I am serious.
Hup two three four.

Actors 1, **3** *and* **4** *start marching.*

Actor 6   Let's go two three four.
Move it two three four.
Hup two three four.

Scene: Presentation [1892]

White Man *and* **Another White Man** *assume a soldierly stance.*

Another White Man   Hup, two, three, four.

Black Man, **Another Black Man**, **Sarah** *and* **Black Woman** *march.*

They might say hups.

Another White Man *watches the training.*

White Man *writes a letter.*

White Man   Dear Sarah.

Another White Man   Straighten the line.

White Man   I'm learning so much here – you will be proud of our work.

Another White Man   Stand up straight.

White Man   The General has picked out a tribe to be in charge of the others.
I am helping to train the leading tribe.

Another White Man   Straight back.

White Man   It is easier for them, as it is easier for us, to be led by one who resembles a better version of our own self.

Another White Man   Yes.

White Man   It is easier for us as well to simplify communications, logistics, organization, etc.

Another White Man   Straight arms.

White Man   In a group of natives –
– a soldier can walk up to the tallest one –

Another White Man   – Stand up straight –

White Man   – with the straightest teeth –

Another White Man   – Straighten the arms –

White Man   – and the fairest skin,
and without a doubt,
address him as leader.

Another White Man   Yes.

White Man   Fair, of course, is a relative term.

Another White Man   Excellent.

White Man   The General is a wise man.

Another White Man   Yes.

White Man   He has worked with natives many times,
and treats them as family.

Another White Man   Good.

White Man   In this assignment,
I am learning how a father must be for his children.

Another White Man   Keep the pace.

White Man   Dear Sarah.
I am thinking of you.

Another White Man   Keep up the pace.

White Man   I am thinking of our future family.

Another White Man *blows a whistle.*

Black Man   Dear Sarah.
I have been craving a fire.
But I don't want a fire that is just a fire.
I want my fire.
I want the fire that holds my ancestors. I want the fire that

I believe in.
I want that fire that makes me believe I know who my
ancestors are – know that they are safe.
I want my belief – my belief that is so strong I search
the desert for trees to burn so that the fire of my ancestors
will never go out.
I have spent my whole life coming home to that fire. And
now.

Another White Man *blows a whistle.*

Another White Man   Railroad building.

Railroad building: **Black Man** *and* **Another Black Man**, **Sarah**
and **Black Woman** *lay tracks. A repetitive, exhausting, physical
gesture. It is percussive in a count of 7 (1-2, 1-2, 1-2-3).*

Black Man   For months I have not built a fire.
For months I have been building
what the Germans call a railroad.
Two straight lines of metal.
The Germans love these straight lines,
Lines of metal, lines of wire, lines of men
Lines and lines and lines and
It seems as though they've always been here.

Another White Man   Keep up the pace.

Scene: Process [1904]

The **Actors** *are stomp-clapping in the other count of 7: (1-2-3,
1-2-3, 1) they have been doing it for a while. Everyone is exhausted.
Irritable.* **Actor 2** *breaks character.* **Actor 3** *is still fully engaged
with the improv, addressing* **Actor 2** *as* **Black Man**.

Actor 2 (*to* **Actor 6**, *if its to anyone*)   It feels like we've been
doing this forever.

Another White Man (*to* **Black Man**)   Keep up the pace.

Actor 2 (*to* **Actor 3**)   I'm not talking to you.

Another White Man   Keep up the pace.

Actor 4/Another Black Man (*to* **Actor 2/Black Man**)   Just keep going.

Actor 2   Or what?

Actor 6 (*a growl at the* **Actors**)   Stay in it.

Actor 2   Why can't we just take a break?

Actor 6   The Herero couldn't just take a break.

Actor 2   I'm not a Herero I'm an actor.

We're due for a break.

Actor 6   We are not taking a break until we are able to do this the way it needs to be done.
So stay in it.

Another White Man (*to* **Black Man**)   We will have a break at the designated time.
Get back into line.

Another Black Man (*to* **Another White Man**)   He's just thirsty.

Actor 2 (*to* **Actor 6**)   Why are we doing this?

Actor 6   For once, can't you just *shut up* and stay in line?

Actor 2   What?

Actor 6   Stay in line!

Actor 2 *storms over to his water.* **Actors** *gradually stop clapping/ stomping as they notice* **Actor 2** *and* **Actor 6**. **Actor 2** *takes a long drink, a deep drink. Or two. The other* **Actors** *watch him, catching their breath.*

Actor 2 *slams his water back down, or throws away his cup. He takes a breath.*

Actor 2   Now I'll get back in line.

Beat.

Actor 6 (*barely controlled*)   When you're trying to make something

Not everyone's going to be happy during every minute of it

But even though we're not comfortable or happy or –

We do stuff we don't want to do because it adds to the greater –

We –

Actor 2   I said I'll get back in line.

Actor 6   That's the thing! You can't just get back in line.

Scene: Presentation [1905]

Chaos. Confusion.

White Man   See you here those assembled.

Your grievances have been heard.

The General has issued a reply.

White Man *and* **Another White Man** *create a wall.*

Actors *might be refugees gathering and fleeing.*

Everything that was in the space gets built up so there is a barricade on one side of the space, and a barren, empty space on the other.

White Man   The letter says

Another White Man   Residents of Sudwestafrika.

White Man   The letter says

Another White Man   Your permission to reside was at the pleasure of the German government.

White Man   The letter says

Another White Man   Your residence no longer pleases the German government.

White Man   The letter says

Another White Man   Your presence will no longer be tolerated.

White Man   The letter says

Another White Man   You have no one to blame but yourselves.

White Man   The letter says

Another White Man   We must set an example, as a father does for his children.

White Man   The letter says

Another White Man   If you are found within our border with guns, you will be shot.

White Man   The letter says

Another White Man   If you are found within our border without guns, you will be shot.

White Man   The letter says

Another White Man   If you are found within our border with cattle, you will be shot.

White Man   The letter says

Another White Man   If you are found within our border without cattle, you will be shot.

White Man   The letter says

Another White Man   We encourage you to move quickly and continuously, for your own safety.

White Man *and* **Another White Man** *salute.* **Another White Man** *marches off.* **White Man** *patrols the wall.* **Black Man** *appears.*

Scene: Process [1905]

Actor 1 *and* **Actor 2** *are thoroughly engaged in an improv, a good improv. A great improv. They are in this moment-to-moment, changing tactics, changing status, raising the stakes, keeping the ball in the air. The characters they play are equally matched – they each flip back and forth between being the aggressor and the victim.*

Actor 1/White Man   You can't come this way.
Are you deaf? I said you can't come through this way.
Are you just going to stand there?
Hey, I said, you just gonna stand there?
Do you plan on answering me?

Actor 2/Black Man   I don't want any trouble.

Actor 1/White Man   I didn't say you did.
You better listen to me.
I am saying this as an order.
An order came down that says that you can't come this
way.

Actor 2/Black Man   My home is that way.

Actor 1/White Man   Well, it says your home can't be this way.

Actor 2/Black Man   But my home is that way.

Actor 1/White Man   If your home stays this way,

He hold his fingers out in the shape of a gun.

I'll have to shoot you.

Actor 2/Black Man (*about the gun*)   I didn't know you had
that.

Actor 1/White Man   Well, I do.
So.

Beat.

Actor 2/Black Man   I have a wife.
Do you have a wife?

Actor 1/White Man   Yeah.

Actor 2/Black Man   I love my wife.
I don't want any trouble.

Actor 1/White Man   I didn't say you did.

Actor 2/Black Man   My home is –

*A slight accent slowly starts to enter **Actor 1**'s diction.*

Actor 1/White Man   Your home is that way now.

Actor 2/Black Man   There is nothing that way.

Actor 1/White Man   That's not true.
Your life is that way.

Actor 2/Black Man   My wife –

Actor 1/White Man   Might just be over that way.

Actor 2/Black Man   You know she's not.

Actor 1/White Man   You don't know that, and neither do I.
She could be –

Actor 2/Black Man   You know she's not.

Actor 1/White Man (*using the gun again*)   I'll shoot you.

A slight accent slowly starts to enter **Actor 2**'*s diction.*

Actor 2/Black Man   Please. I don't want no trouble.

Actor 1/White Man   You keep saying that but –

Actor 2/Black Man (*pacifying*)   Ok.

Actor 1/White Man   Your home is that way.

Actor 2/Black Man   Alright.
I understand.
Just let me go and I'll come right back here –

Actor 1/White Man   No.

Actor 2/Black Man   I say I'll come right back –

Actor 1/White Man   You won't.

Actor 2/Black Man   You have my word.

Actor 1/White Man   You won't come back –

Actor 2/Black Man   I will –

Actor 1/White Man   You won't. Because if you try to come in this direction, I will shoot you.

Actor 2/Black Man   Why can't you let me go? No one will know.

Actor 1/White Man   Might be true.

Actor 2/Black Man   If I go off that way, I will die.

Actor 1/White Man   You might not.

Actor 2/Black Man   What if I run.

Actor 1/White Man   I'm a good shot.

Actor 2/Black Man   I'm a fast runner.

Actor 1/White Man   I'm a great shot.

Actor 2/Black Man   I'm –

Actor 1/White Man   Don't make me shoot you.

Actor 2/Black Man   I'm not making you do anything.

Actor 1/White Man   Do not even take a step over here.

Actor 2/Black Man   You'll shoot me for a step?

Actor 1/White Man   I'll shoot you for breaking the law.

Actor 2/Black Man   I ain't breaking no law –

Actor 1/White Man   Why can't you just respect that I'm telling you the way it is.

Actor 2/Black Man   I'm just tryin' to get home.

Actor 1/White Man   I am trying to help you.

Actor 2/Black Man   You ain't helping no one but yourself.

Actor 1/White Man   Don't you talk to me that way –

Actor 2/Black Man   If you was helping me –

Actor 1/White Man   Don't even know what's good for you –

Actor 2/Black Man   I'd be halfway home by now.

Actor 1/White Man   Don't you take one step.

Actor 2/Black Man   I'm going home.

Actor 1/White Man   Do not –

Actor 2/Black Man   You can't stop me –

Actor 1/White Man   take one step –

Actor 2/Black Man   from going home –

Actor 1/White Man   Don't –

Actor 2/Black Man   You can't stop me –

Actor 1/White Man   Not one step –
Don't –

Actor 2/Black Man *takes a step.*

Actor 1/White Man *immediately shoots him. We hear a loud shot.*

Scene: Presentation [1906]

Black Man *immediately falls. He is still alive. He is breathing. So,* **White Man** *shoots him again.* **Black Man** *is still alive. He is breathing – gasping.* **Black Man** *and* **White Man** *get into a pattern: Breath in. Click. Shot.*

White Man   Dear Sarah.

Black Man (*Breath in.*)

White Man (*Click.*)

(*Shot.*)

White Man   Dear Sarah.

Black Man (*Breath in.*)

White Man (*Click.*)   I'm writing to you today.
Today is a day

(*Shot.*)
Just a day.
Like any day.

Black Man (*Breath in.*)

White Man   Dear Sarah.
(*Click.*)
I'm writing to you today
Today I'm wondering,
Like I've been wondering.
When it's going to rain.
(*Shot.*)
Dear Sarah
People here could use some rain.

Actor 1   Can I have a minute?

Scene: Process

Actor 6   Fine. Take a minute.

Actor 1 *takes a few seconds.*

Actor 1   I can't do this.

Actor 6   You just did.

Actor 1   I can't – I'm not that person.

Actor 2   Neither am I.

Actor 6   Can we help Black Man up people?

Actor 4 *and* **Actor 5** *help* **Actor 2** *up.*

Actor 6   You guys just did some amazing work.
Really great.
But we can't keep stopping like this.
We need to stay in it and move
Or we're never going to figure out this whole genocide
thing.

Actor 1   No. I can't do this.

Actor 6   Yes you can.

Actor 1   I'm not – I'm not the kind of person who could
have done that –

Actor 2   I'm the one that got shot.

Actor 1   But I wouldn't have done that if –

Actor 6   We all know that.
It's just, White Man –

Actor 1   Can you stop calling me White Man?!

Actor 6   No.

Actor 1   I've got a name.

Actor 6   I know.

Actor 1   And if it was me in that situation,
if it was me,
I would have let him go.
I would have.
I wanted to.

Actor 6   So why didn't you?

Actor 1   Because – because that wasn't what happened.
That wasn't what he could have done.

Actor 6   That's right.

Actor 1   And who is that? Who is that person?

Actor 6   That's what we're talking about –

Actor 3   Can I jump in here?
Because, it's like,
I know about this.

Actor 1   Who is that person?

Actor 3   I know about the feelings this character is feeling.
Because, it's like
Ok. So, my father's from America.

Actor 6   We don't have time for this.

Actor 3   Hear me out.
My father's from America and so was his father and his.
And my great-grandfather fought in the Union Army, the
Northern side, in the American Civil War,
And my great-grandfather was in a company from
Pennsylvania
that was made up entirely of coal miners.
Now, I am not a coal miner. I have never been in anything
resembling what you would call a mine, but my great
grand father *was* a coal miner. To the core.
Ha.
Anyway, seriously, listen listen, ok –
So during this one battle, the North and the South were in
a total deadlock for days and days and days, and no one
was gaining any ground, so finally
My grandfather's company were like: um, hello? We're
miners.
So they *mined* underneath the enemy's front-line,
and they packed their mine with gunpowder,
and when the time seemed right,
they blew everything up.

Actor 6   How does this have anything to do with –

Actor 3   I'm getting there.
So the idea had been to blow up the enemy troops
but as they were mining they got lost somehow
got turned around
and instead
they ended up imploding the front-lines of their side
the Union army.
Half of the divisions that made up the Union front fell
through the ground
into this crater.

And the Southern troops charged and broke the Union
line – because the line wasn't a line anymore and
Through the smoke of the molten explosion and the mud
of men and soil and confusion, the enemy troops
got close enough to see
for the first time
the individual men they had been deadlocked with for days.
An entire division of black men
trained by the Union army
fighting in their first battle.
Black men fighting in uniform, as equals.
And to the Southern soldiers, this was like the most
offensive –
I mean the Southerners were fighting for independence
for the right to keep their slaves
And my great-grandfather saw his fellow soldiers not just
being shot,
He saw them being ripped apart in fury.
And my great-grandfather got pinned in a ditch with a
blac – African-American Union soldier, and
As the Southerners got closer and closer,
And my great-grandfather saw the rage in their faces, the
confusion,
So my great-grandfather looked that Union soldier in the
eye
and said 'I'm sorry'. And shot him.
And my great-grandfather saw that that Union soldier
was still alive.
So my great-grandfather shot him again.
And he shot that soldier again,
And again, and
my great-grandfather shot him in fear – out of fear for his
own life and
he shot him so that they would see him shooting him and
he shot him so that he would be captured and kept alive.

Beat.

Actor 2   Are you finished?

Actor 3   (*furious*) Excuse me?

Actor 2   That story doesn't have anything to do with Africa.

Actor 3   It's the same thing –

Actor 4   It's not the same –

| **Actor 6**
This isn't – | **Actor 5**
He's just trying to. |

Actor 3   It's the same dynamic –

Actor 6   This isn't what we should be focusing on –

Actor 4   It's a white man and a black man in America, not –

Actor 2   It's about you instead of us –

Actor 3   My great-grand father –

Actor 2   Again.

Actor 4   There is a difference between here and –

Actor 2   That's your story that's not my story.

Actor 3   I told this deeply personal story because –

Actor 2   All we are doing is hearing the white version of the story / over and over –

Actor 3   The white version?!

Actor 4   He's just saying that you could tell that story / because your grandfather told it to you –

Actor 1   He's never done anything to you.

Actor 6   We're never going to get this done if we keep –

Actor 4   No one is even listening to me.

Actor 5   I am. / I'm listening.

Actor 3   I told that story because we're all trying to understand how someone could do something horrible –

Actor 6   Yes.

Actor 4   And I'm saying that –

Actor 2   I don't want to hear another story about how hard it is to be a white man –

Actor 3/Actor 5   That isn't what I am saying –   / Wait, you guys, listen to –

Actor 2   I don't want to hear anything more from any of you –

Actor 1   You keep putting words in his mouth –

Actor 2   All we do is listen to your version of things over and over and –

Actor 3   Well, [sorry,] but you don't get to tell me what I say / and when I say it –

Actor 2   And I especially don't want to hear you tell some story you just made up –

Actor 3   I didn't make it up.

Actor 2   – so that you can make this all about you –

Actor 3	**Actor 5**
I didn't make it up.	Are you even listening to yourself?

Actor 2   – and tell us your version / of everything when it isn't even about you.

Actor 3	**Actor 5**
That really happened.	Why would he make that up?

Actor 6   We all know it did –

Actor 3   That really happened. I didn't make it up – it's true.

Actor 2   It doesn't matter if it's true or not –

Actor 3   It's not just some story.

Actor 4   None of this is. All of this really happened.

Actor 2   In Africa.

Actor 3   You don't understand.

Actor 2   I'm done with this.

Actor 3   That happened to my family.

Actor 2   I'm done with you.

Actor 3   Actually happened in my family.

Actor 4   And everything we're talking about happened to real people, a whole people, not just one family, thousands of families.

Actor 6   Right – we're talking about something really big here –

Actor 4   An entire tribe of people –

Actor 3   I know I was just –

Actor 1   He knows that we're talking about a genocide.

Actor 6   Tortured, experimented on, enslaved –

Actor 1   Yes a German genocide. A rehearsal Holocaust.

Actor 4   It wasn't a rehearsal.

Actor 1   I know.

Actor 6   It was –

Actor 4   It was real people, in a real place.
It's not a rehearsal if you're actually doing it.

Actor 1	**Actor 5**
I know that.	Of course, but –

Actor 4   And you know what? Not all of the Herero died. Some of them survived.

Actor 1   I didn't mean rehearsal –

Actor 4   Some of them survived their / expulsion into the desert.

Actor 5 (*to* **Actor 1**)   I know.

Actor 4   There are still Herero in the world.

Actor 1   And don't you think it's –
Don't you think it would be offensive to them to have us like
Make up their story for them?

Actor 6   No. I don't think so.

Actor 5   We're just trying to –

Actor 3   We don't have to make it up – we can use our own
stories to –

Actor 5   It can't be offensive if we're all, if we're all just
trying to –

Actor 1   But we didn't find anything about them. Their
stories are gone.

Actor 4   Right. We can use our stories but –

Actor 5   But we're all just trying really hard to understand –

Actor 3   Like some German man has a story just like mine.

Actor 4   Well, we have to be careful –

Actor 3   Right –

Actor 4   Because it's not just –
I mean we could say that there is a *Herero* person
somewhere
that had a story exactly like yours.

Actor 3	**Actor 5**
That's what I'm saying –	And we're trying to –

Actor 4   Where he knows exactly where he's from, and it's
where his father is from, and it's where his grandfather is from –

Actor 3   That is what I'm saying –

Actor 4   But the difference is the Herero man isn't allowed
to go back to his home.

Actor 6   Right.

Actor 4   You can go to America whenever you want
but that Herero man was never able to go back home.
That man knew all of the names of the people who were
killed
and not only that
he knew all of the names of everyone
all of his ancestors
because he believed that they were contained in a sacred fire.

Actor 6   Yes, we know this –

Actor 4   But that fire went out when his grandfather was
forced out of his home,
And when that fire went out his ancestors died.
He believed that his ancestors, all of them,
were murdered because the fire went out.
Can you imagine that?
His entire lineage, all of that history
that was remembered and remembered and remembered
until it was killed
and then it was forgotten.
And I'm not African.
I can't be.
But I know what that is to know that you've lost your heritage,
you've lost the names of your ancestors.

Actor 6 (*fiercely*)   And that is why we need to figure out what
it was like for them.
That is exactly what I have been trying to do since the
very beginning.

Actor 4   But I'm saying that, as British –

Actor 5   As British, we should try to –

Actor 6   No. We keep stopping and we keep talking
and we just need to do it.
So I'm gonna push you to do it so everyone is going to keep
going
And no one is stopping, no one is done nothing is over
because

we're going to stay in it until I say stop.
Ok?
We are going to stay in it until I say stop.
So let's go.
Let's go.
1905.
The wall has been erected.
One hundred and fifty miles wide.
On one side, there is home. On the other side, there is
desert.
Black Man, you've been in the desert for days without
anything to drink.
Go.

Scene: Processtation

Actor 2   There must be some water somewhere.

Beat.

Actor 4 (*jumping in, eventually*)   The Germans have poisoned
the watering holes.

Actor 6   Yes, the guards made to stand the line were
ordered to shoot on sight.

Actor 2   So, get down.

Actor 4   Oh I didn't realise –

Actor 2   Get down.

They're on the ground.

Actor 4/Another Black Man   I'm thirsty.
Maybe it will rain soon?

Actor 2   In the middle of the desert?

Actor 4/Another Black Man   Yeah.

Actor 2   I don't think so.

Beat.

Actor 4/Another Black Man   Did you feel that?

Actor 2   What?

Actor 4/Another Black Man   I think I felt a drop of rain.

Actor 2   You didn't feel anything.

Actor 4/Another Black Man   You know what? I just felt another drop.

Actor 2   Stop it.

Actor 6   [No, keep going.]

Actor 4/Another Black Man   I felt it! A drop of rain.

Actor 2/Black Man Ok.

Actor 4/Another Black Man   Did you feel it? I felt it, so you must have felt it.

Actor 2/Black Man   You're hallucinating.

Another Black Man   No. You can feel it.
Cool clear water, pouring down from the sky.

Actor 2/Black Man   I think I heard thunder.

Another Black Man   A roar of thunder. A clap of lightning.

Black Man   I can't even hear you over the storm.

Another Black Man   I'm soaked right down to the bone.
I can feel the rain on my tongue.

Black Man   Dear Sarah.
I have been waiting for you to arrive.

Black Woman/Actor 6   I will arrive and it will rain.
We will collect the rain in our clothes,

Black Man   and skin and hair,

Black Woman/Actor 6   and we will walk across the desert

Black Man   and when we get thirsty

Black Woman/Actor 6   we will hold our clothes and skin and hair to our mouths and be refreshed.

Black Man   Dear dear Sarah. She's so right.

Actor 6   You can see them

White Man/Actor 1   Yes.

Actor 6   You can see them. And you know it's not raining.

White Man/Actor 1   Yes.

Actor 6   You can see them. And what did the General say? You know what the General said.

White Man, Another White Man *and* **Sarah**   The General said,
Within the German Borders,
Every Herero,
Whether armed or unarmed,
With or without cattle,
Will be shot.

Actor 6   And where are we.

White Man, Another White Man *and* **Sarah**   Sudwestafrika.

Actor 6   This is Germany.
The General has made this Germany.
And they are rebels.
They have started a rebellion that has raged on for years.
They have forced you to be here for years.
You have been standing on this wall for years.
They have threatened your lives.
Now you have orders.
You have new orders.
What are your orders?

White Man, Another White Man *and* **Sarah**   We are to round them up.
We are to chain them up.
We are to lead them up to the camp.

We are to imprison them there.
We are to keep our country safe for our countrymen.
We are to control them to keep the safety.

Actor 6   Round them up.
Chain them up.
Lead them up.
Lock them up.

White Man, **Another White Man** *and* **Sarah** *pick up and
continue* **Actor 6***'s chant.*

White Man *and* **Another White Man** *are leading* **Black Man**
and **Another Black Man** *to begin hard labour. It turns into a
song. A work song. A slave song. Accents creep in as the song is sung
and the chant is chanted.*

White Man, Another White Man [Sarah]	**Black Man, Another Black Man [Black Woman]**
Round 'em up.	*Take me to my home*
Chain 'em up.	*Take me to that place*
Lead 'em up.	*Place that I am from*
Lock 'em up.	*Take me to my home*
(repeat)	*Home that ain't my home*
	Where do I belong
	Took me from my home
	Place where I belong
	Place that's now your home
	Where I don't belong –

Black Man   I don't belong here.

Another White Man   You can't just stop.

Black Man   I ain't supposed to be here.

Another White Man (*referring to* **Another Black Man**)   You
got that one?

White Man   Yeah. You better not give me no trouble.

Another White Man   Now where you think you going to
run to?

Black Man   I ain't supposed to be here.

Another White Man   I ain't supposed to be here either.

Black Man   You bessa let me go.

Another White Man   That ain't how this works, boy.

Black Man *pushes* **Another White Man** *aside, and goes towards exit.*

Another White Man   You better / come back here.
You better get right back here.
You are breaking the law right now.

White Man   You move and I'll shoot you, you hear me?
I will shoot you and you better believe I won't blink an eye.

White Man *and* **Another White Man** *catch* **Black Man**.

Black Man   You bessa take your hand off me.

Another White Man   You shut the fuck up.
Sit down.

White Man   Sit down.
Sit your ass down, you do what I tell you.

Actor 2/Black Man *goes to hit* **White Man**.

White Man   You gonna hit me, or you gonna sit?

The scene continues.

White Man   Now answer me this.
You know what you done?

Another White Man   What are you asking him for?
I know what he done.
He trespassed, he stole from the government.
He assaulted me.

White Man   You know what that means?
That means you broke the law.

Black Man   I ain't broke no law.

White Man   You don't talk back to me, boy.

Black Man   I said –

Another White Man   Don't you lie, boy. You lie again, I'll cut your tongue, you son of a bitch.
You broke the law.
Say it.

Another White Man *lands blows on* **Black Man** *on each 'Tell'*.

Another White Man   Tell the man you broke the law.
Tell the man you tried to put your hands on me.
Tell the man before I Tell him for you.
Tell the man you tried to kill me.
Tell the man you were gonna kill me.
I don't need you to Tell me that you were gonna kill me.
I can Tell you wanted to kill me so Tell the man.
Tell him.
Tell him.

Black Man *pushes back. A struggle.*

Black Man *knocks* **White Man** *down.*

White Man   You better run, nigger.
I said run.
Run, nigger.

Black Man *runs.*

Black Man / **Ensemble** (*under his breath, in a rhythm of 7: 1-2-3, 1-2-3, 1*)   Running. Running. Run running. Running. Run.

Black Man *runs. The* **Ensemble** *blocks him.*

White Man *and* **Another White Man** *chase.*

They catch him.

Another White Man   What do you want to do with him?

White Man   I got to think.

White Man *and* **Another White Man** *bind him.*

A beat of 7 continues – a stomp/clap – stomps on the down beats, claps in between. The women are the source. 1-2, 1-2, 1-2-3.

Another White Man   We got to do our order.

White Man   Let's see it.

A letter is handed to **White Man**. *He shows it to* **Black Man**.

White Man   You know what this means?
Do you know what this means?
I'll show you what this means.

He rips the letter. He rips holes for eyes. He rips a hole for a mouth. He has made a crude mask. He holds it in front of **Black Man**'*s face. The audience is part of the crowd.*

White Man   You understand what this is now?

He sticks the mask onto **Black Man**'*s face.*

White Man   You understand what this is now?

He pretends his arms are **Black Man**'*s arms. He pretends to be*

Black Man.

White Man (*as* **Black Man**)   Oh I understands!
You is gonna kill me.
But you bessa be careful, white man.
Cause Lawd knows I is gonna haunt you.
I's gonna be a ghost prince of Africa!
I's gonna scream like my brother jungle apes!
Oooga booga!

Another White Man   Oooh, I am terrified!

White Man   Oooga booga!

Another White Man   Oooga booga!

White Man   Oooga booga boo!

The beat of 7 grows even louder. Their words become chants or song. Eventually their movements become dance. Eventually the entire ensemble share the chants/song/dance. They feel the rhythm for dance and speech/song in measures of 7.

7a: 1-2, 1-2, 1-2 -3:

Another White Man
Ooogaaa booga
Ooogaaa booga
Ooogaaa booga

Another White Man	**White Man**
Ooogaaa booga	I black man
Ooogaaa booga	I black man
Ooogaaa booga	Remember
Ooogaaa booga	Africa

Another White Man	**White Man**	**Black Man**
Ooogaaa booga	I am man from	I am a black man I have
Ooogaaa booga	Africa and	been a black man always I
Ooogaaa booga	I alone can	remember what it was to
Ooogaaa booga	Remember the	be a man alone I am
Ooogaaa booga	Africa that	a black man I have been a
Ooogaaa booga	I was from	black man always black always

7b: 1-2-3, 1-2-3, 1:

All   Running. Running. Run running. Running. Run. Running. Running. Run running. Running. Run.

7a: 1-2, 1-2, 1-2-3:

Another Black Man	**Sarah**	**White Men**
When they first came they called me prince		
called me leader	They	
of all people.	They	

Another Black Man	Sarah	White Men
They called me straight	They	Straight
straightest, straight back	They	Straight straight
straight teeth. Straight was	They	Straight
the best to them:	They	Straight straight
straight lines, straight seams,	They	Straight
straight gaze ahead,	They	Straight straight
straight heads of hair.	They	Straight

7b: 1-2-3, 1-2-3, 1:

Black Man	All Others
I have been black all my life	Running. Running. Run
I have been black all my life	running. Running. Run
I have been black all my life	running. Running. Run
I have been black all my life	running. Running. Run

Cheers.

7a: 1-2, 1-2, 1-2-3:

Another White Man   I heard a joke once.
How come all the damn
Niggers that we see
Can run so damn fast?
Cause the slow niggers
Are locked up in jail.

7b: 1-2-3, 1-2-3, 1:

Black Man	All Others
I have been black all my life	Running. Running. Run
I have been black all my life	running. Running. Run

Cheers.

7b: 1-2, 1-2, 1-2-3:

White Man   I heard a joke once.
How do you stop a
Nigger from going out?
Pour more gas on him.

7b: 1-2-3, 1-2-3, 1:

Black Man	**All Others**
I have been black all my life	Running. Running. Run
I have been black all my life	Running. Running. Run

7a: 1-2, 1-2, 1-2-3:

Another White Man   I heard a joke once.
If you throw a nigger
And a jew
Off a roof
Which one is going to land first?
The nigger lands first
Because shit falls faster than ashes.

7b: 1-2-3, 1-2-3, 1:

Black Man	**All Others**
I have been black all my life	Running. Running. Run
I have been black all my life	running. Running. Run

7a: 1-2, 1-2, 1-2-3: **White Man** *tops* **Another White Man***'s joke.*

White Man   I heard a joke once –

Punch-line: **White Man** *shows off a noose.*

7b: 1-2-3, 1-2-3, 1:

All Others   Running. Running. Run
running. Running. Run
running. Running. Run
running. Running. Run

White Man *and* **Another White Man**   *put the noose around*
Black Man's *neck and throw it over a beam or branch. They*
threaten and terrify him, and enjoy his fear. **Black Man** *breaks*
character.

Actor 2   Help me.
Seriously.
Help me.
Get this fucking thing off me.

Actor 6 *eventually helps* **Actor 2**.

Actor 2   Get this thing off me.
Get this fucking thing off me.
Get this thing off me.
Get this thing off me.

Actor 6   You're ok. It's off. You're ok.

A silence. **Actor 2** *leaves the stage.* **Actor 6** *leaves after him.*
Silence.

And in that silence something starts to happen. The actors start to
process what just happened. And there is something . . . Discomfort.
Frustration. Awkwardness. Nerves. Adrenaline. Uncertainty.
Buzzing. Embarrassment. Guilt. Shame. Anger. Excitement.
Something . . . Which might lead to a smile. Which might lead to
laughter.

If it does, **Actors 5**, **3** *and* **1** *find laughter. The laughter starts and*
stops. There might be failed attempts to shake off the moment in the
laughter. There might be failed attempts to congratulate each other in
the laughter. There might be failed imitations of the performance in
the laughter. There might be failed explanations in the laughter.
There might be failed attempts to stop laughing in the laughter.

They might laugh and cry, they might laugh and scream, they might laugh and be silent, they might laugh and rip things apart. They might laugh and break. The actors might break, the moment might break, the momentum might break, the play might lose control, but the performers cannot stop until there is laughter, and it is genuine. The performers say and do whatever is in their minds.

But **Actor 4** *is not laughing. He might try. But he cannot laugh. He cannot leave. As the other* **Actors** *have their reaction,* **Actor 4** *eventually notices the audience. And then . . .*

Actor 4   *cleans up the space.* **Actors 5, 3** *and* **1** *see* **Actor 4***. It jolts them out of whatever they were in. They watch him clean up the space.*

He picks up objects that have come to hold significance: Bottles of water, the bits of the mask, etc. And places them in the box of letters.

Actors 5, 3 *and* **1** *eventually remember the audience, and take them in, or they just remember* **Actor 4***, or they remember themselves. In this remembering, they might be forced to leave the space.*

Actor 4 *takes down the noose. It is the last object to be dealt with.*

He puts it in or on the box of letters, the archive. He closes the box.

He looks to the audience.

He tries to say something to the audience but . . .

He might produce the air of a word beginning with the letter 'w' like 'We' or 'Why' or 'What'.

He tries to speak, but he fails.

End of play.

Addendum

Felt in 7a: 1-2, 1-2, 1-2-3

Beats /Parts	1	2	3	4	5	6	7
Another White Man		Ooo		Gaaa		Boo	Ga
White Man	**I**		**Black**		**Man**		
	I		**Black**		**Man**		
	Re		**mem**		**ber**		
	Af		**ri**		**ca**		
	I		**am**		**man**		from
	Af		**ri**		**ca**		and
	I		**a**		**lone**		can
	Re Af		**mem**		**ber**		The
	I		**ri**		**ca**		that
			was		**from**		
Black Man	**I**	am	**a**	black	**man**	I	Have
	Been	a	**black**	man	**al**	ways	I
	Re	mem	**ber**	what	**it**	was	To
	Be	a	**man**	a	**lone**	I	Am
	A	black	**man**	I	**have**	been	A
	Black	man	**al**	ways	**black**	al	Ways

Felt in 7b: 1-2-3, 1-2-3, 1

Beats/Parts	1	2	3	4	5	6	7
Ensemble	**Runn-**	-ing		**Runn-**	ing		**Run**
	I	have	been	**black**	all	my	**life**

Felt in 7a: 1-2, 1-2, 1-2-3

Beats/Parts	1	2	3	4 5	6	7
Another Black Man		When	**they**		first	came
		they	**called**		me	prince

Called	**me**	lead	er
of	**all**	peo	ple
They	**called**	me	straight
straight	**est**	Straight	back
straight	**teeth**	straight	was
the	**best**	to	them
Straight	**lines**	straight	seams
Straight	**gaze**	a	head
Straight	**heads**	of	hair

Ensemble   **They**

Ensemble   Straight
                                                                   Straight

        straight

Felt in 7b: 1-2-3, 1-2-3, 1

Beats/Parts	**1**	2	3	**4**	5	6	**7**
Ensemble	**Runn-**	-ing		**Runn-**	ing		**Run**
	I	have	been	**black**	all	my	**life**

9 781350 146402